Christmas is coming, the goose is getting fat
Please to put a penny in the old man's hat;
If you haven't got a penny, a ha'penny will do,
If you haven't got a ha'penny then God bless you!

Anon. | Traditional nursery rhyme

For my lovely Ma, Polly,
who loved Christmas so.
It's not the same without you.

CHRISTMAS
is
COMING

Auriol Bishop

Text copyright © 2023 Auriol Bishop

Illustrations on pages i, iii, 11, 18, 19, 118, 124, 125, 250, 251, 312 © 2023 Lucy Rose
Illustrations on pages 41, 98, 155, 238 © Tartila/Shutterstock
All other illustrations © 2023 Auriol Bishop

The right of Auriol Bishop to be identified as the Author of
the Work has been asserted by her in accordance with the
Copyright, Designs and Patents Act 1988.

First published in 2023 by Headline Home
an imprint of Headline Publishing Group

2

Apart from any use permitted under UK copyright law, this publication may only be reproduced, stored,
or transmitted, in any form or by any means, with prior permission in writing of the publishers or, in the case of
reprographic production, in accordance with the terms of licences issued by the Copyright Licensing Agency.

Every effort has been made to fulfil requirements with regard to reproducing copyright material.
The author and publisher will be glad to rectify any omissions at the earliest opportunity.

Cataloguing in Publication Data is available from the British Library

Hardback ISBN 978 1 0354 0639 5
eISBN 978 1 0354 0640 1

Publishing Director: Lindsey Evans
Senior Editor: Kate Miles
Copy Editor: Sophie Elletson
Proofreaders: Jill Cole and Margaret Gilbey
Indexer: Ruth Ellis

Typeset by EM&EN
Printed and bound in Great Britain by Clays Ltd, Elcograf S.p.A.

Headline's policy is to use papers that are natural, renewable and recyclable products and made from
wood grown in well-managed forests and other controlled sources. The logging and manufacturing processes
are expected to conform to the environmental regulations of the country of origin.

HEADLINE PUBLISHING GROUP
An Hachette UK Company
Carmelite House
50 Victoria Embankment
London EC4Y 0DZ

www.headline.co.uk
www.hachette.co.uk

~ Contents ~

Introduction		1
	About this Book	4
	The True Meaning of Christmas (to you)	10
	Christmas Beliefs & Traditions	11
I	September ~ Gathering	17
	Christmas Kit	22
	September's Special Days	33
	September/October Festivals that move with the Moon	47
II	October ~ Preparation	63
	Christmas Cooking	68
	October's Special Days	79
	October/November Festivals that move with the Moon	109
III	November ~ Anticipation	123
	Presents	128
	Christmas Card Etiquette	136
	Party Season	138
	November's Special Days	145
	November/December Festivals that move with the Moon	169

IV	December ~ Celebration	181
	Decking the Halls	186
V	Advent	193
VI	Christmas Day	251
VII	The Twelve Days of Christmas	257
	Author's Note	290
	Acknowledgements	293
	Bibliography	295
	Endnotes	301
	Index	306

HRISTMAS has its roots deep in the prehistoric past, with our ancestors of the Northern Hemisphere finding hope in the darkest times of the year.

It is named for a man from the desert lands many centuries past, remembered by millions across the world as prophet and saviour.

More recently, tradition has sprinkled Christmas with snowflakes and icing sugar, weaving glittering tinsel amongst the ancient Yuletide evergreens.

This little book is a celebration of all we share, across time and across cultures and continents.

From the equinox to Twelfth Night, each page holds something to unwrap: a little piece of history, or inspiration, things you might like to make or cook or do, and sometimes just a quiet thought to bring you peace.

Introduction

— *ntroduction* —

I grew up in the English countryside, where winter was a time of old man's beard and teasels, sloe-picking and bonfires, icy puddles and the magical lace of spiders' webs crystallised with frost.

My mother adored Christmas.

She made it a time of parties and parlour games, transforming our house into a palace of greens and reds and golds; natural candlelight and evergreens; rich homemade fruitcake and mulled wine kept warm by a blazing open fire.

She threw lavish entertainments on a tight budget and loved nothing more than dressing up and dining well, surrounded by interesting people, dear friends and her beloved family.

This book is a tribute to her, to the wonder she brought to us each year in the darkest months.

Nowadays, I live in London, which brings its own brand of festive magic.

Our suburban neighbourhood booms with fireworks for Diwali, and local children go wild with pagan excitement on Hallowe'en.

Then comes the thrill when the lights go up, strung high over iconic shopping streets with windows bedecked in miniature stageshows of seasonal delights.

Christmas markets sell glühwein and lebkuchen on the banks of the river, and office parties spill out from restaurants celebrating culinary cultures from every corner of the world.

We can fly overnight from winter to summer and back again, and the mind-boggling devices in our pockets have the power to show us, in real time, that even as we cosy up for the long, dark nights, our friends are rejoicing in the sun.

And I'm learning that this time of year has as many meanings as there are people in the world.

~ About this Book ~

Part almanac, part anthology and part guide, this little companion for Christmas begins with the equinox – and through September, October and November, picks out the special days. From December, it's an Advent calendar of a book, with something for every day in the countdown to Christmas Day, and for the Twelve Days of Christmas beyond.

I've filled it with the traditions I've inherited from my mother, the ones I've created in my own life, and the wonderful things I'm discovering and learning from all over the world.

You'll find poems and extracts from classic stories, inspiration for things you might like to make or cook or do. But most of all, I hope you'll find a little escape from the cacophony that Christmas can be.

Rather than adding to your to-do list, I want these pages to bring you comfort, and reassurance that the only perfect Christmas is the one that feels perfect to you.

When you revel in your favourite memories of this time of year, what is it that you love most?

How we celebrate Christmas – how we want to celebrate – is deeply personal. Even when we share cultural traditions, we will have different childhood memories, family circumstances and personal tastes in what we value, love and hate about the season.

Whether you're a party animal or love that it's the best binge-watching-TV day of the year, that's okay. And while we sometimes feel bound by traditions, it's okay to set yourself free, too: be somewhere different, or have a quiet one, release yourself from obligations and see what that looks like. Think about what you would like to make time for, if you can.

And remember, it's a time for loving and giving. You don't have to be the one who does it all. Delegate, share things out. Be like the angels and work together.

~

For me, the practicalities of Christmas – well, any celebration really – can be encapsulated in two things: the treats and the decorations. And you can make those two things as simple or as complicated as you like.

Perhaps you're a Mother Christmas, with store-cupboards crammed with special Christmas things; or an Elf, who starts making elaborate plans for next year the instant this one is done; or perhaps you're more like me, who loves the idea of Christmas but somehow it always comes much more quickly than I think and when it does, I haven't done half of what I planned. I hope you're more the way I'd like to be, and do the things you love, with the people you love, and enjoy whatever comes. Because, really, pretty much whatever you do, at this time of year it becomes Christmassy. I mean, you can buy Christmas loo roll if you want to. There's no escape from the festive magic!

So, in the pages ahead you'll find an introduction to each month that tells us what Mother Christmas and the Elves are up to. As well as inspiration for the 'Special Days' with dates set on the Gregorian calendar from 20 September through to 7 January, you'll find a section for what's happening in the lunar months: the festivals that move with the Moon.

Dip in, and find what speaks to you . . .

It's the most wonderful time
of the year!

Slow down and savour it.

Seek out the signs of the shifting seasons.

Wrap up in traditions old and new,
revel in memories and look up at the sky full of stars
we all share.

And the angel said unto them,
   'Fear not: for, behold, I bring you good tidings of great joy, which shall be to all people.'

Luke 2:10

Before it all begins, take a moment to yourself. Sit in your favourite spot, treat yourself to your favourite drink, and think:

What, for you, are the essential ingredients of Christmas?

Depending on where you are in the world, it could be about cosying up or hitting the beach.

The most important thing is that it holds what's special for you, and what you most need from this time of the year.

Think about why it all began, with our ancestors looking for hope in the dark days of winter, wanting to express their gratitude for the light and warmth of the sun.

The most important gift you can give to yourself and to everyone around you is: find what brings comfort and joy, and put that at the heart of everything . . .

~ The True Meaning of Christmas (to you) ~

This is an important time of year for many faiths and cultures – Christmas isn't the only significant festival to fall within these months.

Some are celebrations of the natural world or hopes for auspicious planting and harvest times; some are theological: religious observations and reminders of our place in a cosmos so much bigger than ourselves.

Whatever the belief in our hearts, it seems we share so much in the ways we express our joy and gratitude and humility. The traditions of spiritual contemplation, community, charity, gifts and feasting are universal.

And then, of course, there are our individual rituals: the things we always do each year, or something we did for the first time that was so special we hope to do it again and again. The things we inherit, or discover from new friends, or adopt as we experience cultures different from our own. The weird and quirky ways we celebrate that only a handful of those closest to us will ever understand.

This is 'the true meaning' of these festive days. What is important to you? Why is this time so special? What is your heritage? And what do you want to pass on?

Christmas Beliefs & Traditions

Christmas wouldn't be Christmas without a list – so let's start with a little alphabet of all things naughty and nice . . . !

Angels
Guardians, messengers, bringers of glad tidings of great joy.

Baby Jesus
Christkind, Christ child and also sometimes the bringer of presents and the Christmas tree.

Bells
Church bells, jingle bells, sleigh bells. The sound of Little Jesus letting us know our presents are here at last – or of an angel getting their wings.

Bethlehem
'House of Bread', 'House of Meat': a desert outpost town famous for its wheat and fertile farmlands. Home of the Church of the Nativity, with its small 'door of humility' – and a surprising Christmas tradition of bagpipe band parades. The holy family's journey to Bethlehem and search for a place to stay is re-enacted in the Latin American tradition of Las Posadas processions from house to house in the nine nights before Christmas. The Aramaic greeting – in the language of Jesus – is *Eedookh Breekha*, 'Blessed be your Christmas.'

Camels
Traditional mounts of the three kings, bearing gifts. They like grass or straw and appreciate a bucket of water . . .

Carols
Bright-faced community choirs with a collecting tin, shuffling cheeky kids squeaking on the doorstep, the single pure voice of a choir boy that somehow fills an entire cathedral. Whether you find yourself humming that little festive refrain under your breath or have been practising your solo since September, there's just no escaping.

Christmas tree
A towering gift between nations, centrepiece of town square or sitting room. Twinkling with faux candlelight or flashing corner disco, artfully designed in this year's colour scheme or a miniature family museum of handmade ornaments only a mother could love. Sometimes delivered by Santa Claus, or Little Jesus, or the angels. Nothing smells like a real Christmas tree.

Dreaming of a white Christmas
It takes the sighting of just a single snowflake for the UK Met Office to declare a white Christmas, and snow is not impossible in Bethlehem – but the snowy vision depicted on Christmas cards is only guaranteed on mountain tops and in the far Northern Hemisphere. For everywhere else, snowflakes are paper, snowballs are for drinking, and snowmen sometimes built of sand. Capture your snow-filled dreams with icing peaks on Christmas cakes, hot chocolate topped in wild whirls of whipped cream, drifts of pavlova meringue, icicle edging around gingerbread rooftops and flurries of icing sugar. The wonders of modern technology make it possible – and magical – to go ice skating in the most unlikely places; but for skiing, tobogganing and sleigh rides you really need to go to the snow.

Elves
Santa's little helpers: you'd better be nice or they might steal you away!

Father Christmas
Sinterklaas, St Nicholas, Small Nicholas, Father Frost, Good Old Man, Yule Man, Grandfather Snow, Old Man Winter, Christmas Man . . .

He's sometimes accompanied by present-giving angels and coal-bringing devils, 'the trotters' who scare bad children, or his granddaughter the Snow Maiden. He's also known to travel with his side-kick Sooty Peter, who does the dirty work of climbing down the chimney – and might snatch naughty children away in his sack. I much prefer the sound of his other assistant Krampus, who leaves golden twigs as a reminder to behave.

Christmas goat
Joulupukki is a rarer Christmas creature than some others and is less scary these days than the beast of long ago: over time he has mellowed from demanding presents to being the gift-giver himself, and is more human than goat – but you still have to be careful to keep him happy, or all you'll find under the tree is a bag of coal! Prankster goats are also to be found causing trouble amongst the carol-singers. Beware . . .

Midnight Mass
Misa de Gallo, Mass of the Rooster.
The greatest mystery revealed in the dead of night. Candles and incense and the great swelling of song. Tumbling home afterwards for feasting and fireworks and gifts if you're good!

Mistletoe
Every berry the promise of a kiss!

Nativity ~ scenes, plays, processions . . .

A cave, a bed of straw, and the shepherds who arrived long before the kings: Christ's birth is a story of inclusivity and humble beginnings.

There are wonderful tales from around the world about who visits the baby Jesus in his manger each year. Alongside the little donkey, the oxen and sheep, you might spot flamingoes or llamas; and far in the corner behind the butcher, baker, policeman and priest squats El Caganer the Catalonian pooping man.

Decorate your nativity scene with flowers and fruit – even letters to the Christchild who may bring you presents on Christmas Day.

Novena

Prayers, carols and food with family and friends for nine contemplative nights before Christmas.

Processions, performances ~ and pantomime!

A donkey stopping traffic on the city streets, children's eyes shining with light from the lanterns they've made, carnival floats that take all year to build. Terrible puns and predictable plots. Dancing, singing, drumming that builds and thrums until the hearts of everyone in the whole world seem to beat the same beat.

Reindeer

Back when he was Old Father Christmas, Santa rode a horse (and Sinterklaas still does) but these days he's more often seen in his sleigh. Either way, it's good to leave out some hay and carrots, maybe even special oats, alongside the treats for Father Christmas.

Shepherds
Heroes of the nativity, in some places they even have their own pastorelas – plays – and inspire Father Christmas's traditional dress.

Shoes, boots, socks and stockings
Give them a good clean and leave them out in the right place at the right time, and who knows what you might find in the morning?

Stars
Guiding the way and topping the tree, lighting windows and carol-singers. Twinkling signs that the night's celebrations are ready to begin.

Three Wise Men
The feast of the kings, Epiphany, is the climax of Christmas. Gaspar King of Sheba brings frankincense, Melchior King of Arabia brings gold, Balthazar King of Tarsus and Egypt brings myrrh. Leave out your shoes on Epiphany Eve, with some treats for the kings (they're partial to satsumas and walnuts, I hear), and if you've been good they'll bring gifts for you, too. Apparently, even the coal you get for being naughty is made of sugar . . .

Yule log
Cut specially from oak or elm, cherry or pear tree and sometimes sprinkled with red wine, to burn in the hearth from Christmas Eve until Epiphany. Or delicious bûche de Noël chocolate Swiss roll cake. Take good care of your Tio de Nadal Christmas log, tucking it up in a blanket and feeding it little titbits, and you might get some treats in return.

Kicking through leaves on crisp sunny days, conker hunting and the sudden honking vee of geese migrating overhead. Seed-heads clattering in the autumn breeze. Sharp apples eaten straight from the tree, and blackberry crumble the sweet reward for an afternoon of scrambling through brambles.

September is a time for foraging and bottling, pickling and fermenting. Doing the little things we'll be glad of later. Or perhaps it's simply a moment to gather ourselves, to pause and notice the changes in the air.

'**What is it,** my sweetheart?' said Mother. 'You don't feel ill, do you?'

'I don't know,' Bobbie answered, a little breathlessly, 'but I want to be by myself and see if my head really IS all silly and my inside all squirmy-twisty.'

'Hadn't you better lie down?' Mother said, stroking her hair back from her forehead.

'I'd be more alive in the garden, I think,' said Bobbie. But she could not stay in the garden. The hollyhocks and the asters and the late roses all seemed to be waiting for something to happen. It was one of those still, shiny autumn days, when everything does seem to be waiting.

Bobbie could not wait.

E. Nesbit | *from* The Railway Children

SEPTEMBER will always feel like back-to-school for me. It used to be a time of new uniforms, a new pencil case, new rules to learn and sometimes new people to get along with. And still these days it seems a time of gathering. A moment to collect myself and regroup before the pace picks up in earnest again.

I resolve that this year I will make all my Christmas presents, send cards out in November, plan ahead and keep things simple. Maybe just this once I'll manage to be organised and have everything done in good time so I can relax and enjoy the December days when they come.

Mother Christmas makes warming porridge for frosty mornings and busily sews on nametapes and darns socks and checks we have shoes, clothes that fit, everything we need for the new season. She starts reading wine reviews and recipes, keeping an eye out for special offers on the pricey things that can be bought now and kept for later. She turns down pages in the special festive edition magazines and catalogues that start tumbling through the door, collecting ideas and inspiration in a glossy pile beside her chair.

The elves start planning: what needs to happen and when in the weeks and months ahead. There are checklists and calendars, maybe even a spreadsheet or ingenious new productivity app. Dates are made and timings are plotted. Who needs to be where and do what is all agreed and noted down. The address book is up to date, in a handy digital format that is easy to print out as labels.

I have to confess I'm too distracted by conkers for any of that – how is it that they're so shiny?

I can't resist: acorn cups and sycamore propellers and a rainbow of turning leaves find their way into my pockets, and all feels well with the world . . .

Christmas Kit ~ Gathering What You Need

DIY and cleaning might not be the first thing you think of when you think of Christmas, and yet it's one of the most universal traditions: to prepare your home ahead of any festival, to make bright, clean, welcoming spaces and invest in the things that will help you live comfortably and well.

Dhanteras, the first day of Diwali celebrations which will be coming up in October/November, is considered an auspicious day for buying new kitchen appliances – including a broom to sweep out poverty and negativity – and legends suggest you fill new utensils with food or water before you step inside the house, to ensure they will be filled all year long.

As we think about gathering what we need in September, perhaps it's a good moment to have a look at what we have, what we want – and what might go on the Christmas wish list.

Mother Christmas and the Elves have likely packed away their Christmas things in an orderly fashion, ready to be easily found and brought out as and when they are needed. And, of course, they are fully prepared with DIY and kitchen things all year round.

Personally, I find the pressure to keep on top of housework quite stressful, mainly because I always forget to allow enough time for it. I aspire to (but confess I am very far from achieving!) the Japanese art of *seiso* – daily cleaning to enjoy your space and discover hidden problems. Knowing I have the kit I need can really help.

Advent kit

Anything you need for your Advent rituals: calendars, candles, the little decorative touches you like to dot about. I have Christmas-spiced door hangers, frankincense and myrrh-infused golden potpourri, embroidered hand towels, all gifts from Christmases past that I like to get out for the first day of December.

Bedding kits

Are you likely to have people coming to stay over the season? Do you have places for them to sleep? Bedding? Towels?
Here's a tip my friend taught me: gather together sleep kits. Use a pillowcase as a bag to hold everything else: sheet, duvet cover, guest towel, etc. Pop in a lavender bag to keep it smelling sweet, and if you want to be fancy-festive, you could even tie it up with a ribbon and put a tag on it so you remember what's in there.

Then when you're getting things ready for your guests, all you have to do is grab a kit and make up the bed – or even better, hand it over to them to do!

Bin bags and cleaning kit

You can go all fancy and treat yourself to an Insta-worthy enamelled caddy if you like, but really you just need a handy grab-bag that's easily accessible without spoiling the elegant Christmas decor vibes:

- ☆ Cloths to mop up emergency spills
- ☆ Dustpan and brush
- ☆ Rubber gloves
- ☆ Biodegradable bags you can just shove full of rubbish and get out into the bin as quickly as possible

- ☆ Clothes brush/pet-hair brush/one of those natty little carpet-scraper devices brilliant for brushing up hair
- ☆ Tissues for the inevitable snotty victims of whatever seasonal lurgy is going around (and their own personal bin bag so you don't have to deal with the aftermath)
- ☆ Plenty of toilet roll (don't stockpile, that's selfish; just one more pack than you'd normally buy will do)

The most important thing is: make sure *everyone* knows where to find this kit, not just you: they spill it, they mop it up!

Christmas cards and crackers

They don't go off, so are something you can buy in the sales or keep a stock of for next year. Likewise little presents. Just make sure to store them with your Advent kit, so you remember that you have them . . .

Christmas cooking kit

- ☆ Mixing bowl and spoon
- ☆ A whisk is also handy
- ☆ Baking trays, cake tins, Swiss roll tins, mince pie tins, cookie cutters – if you like to get baking
- ☆ Small pan and a bowl that fits on top, for melting chocolate, etc.
- ☆ Roasting tin, pie tin or loaf tin for whatever meat/fish/pastry/nut roast centrepiece you have planned
- ☆ Another roasting tin, for potatoes and veg
- ☆ Large lidded pan or casserole to cook up red cabbage, soups, porridge, rice pudding

If you have festive tea towels, oven gloves, aprons, fridge magnets, cookery books, etc., keep them in your Advent kit.

Christmas-decoration-hanging kit

- ☆ Wire + wire cutter
- ☆ Those little wire bauble hanger things, or bent-open paper clips do the job just as well
- ☆ Light-weight hammer and tacks that won't leave massive holes in the plaster
- ☆ Drawing pins
- ☆ String/wire twists/cable ties (string or wire is best unless there is such a thing as biodegradable/recyclable cable ties these days)
- ☆ Step ladder (I know you will probably ignore me and teeter precariously on an unsuitable stool like you usually do, but really a ladder is best if you don't want to ruin your skiing plans by breaking a limb before you even hit the slopes)

Christmas dinner/party kit

If you have the luxury of storage space, you may have, or find in the sales and charity shops, or be given, any number of special serving and table-scaping things. My friend and I have a tradition of giving each other fancy paper serviettes each year, so I know I always have that covered. Get a reputation for your love of Christmas things, and it becomes an easy present. Crockery, serving dishes, tablecloths, runners, napkins, candlesticks, cocktail glasses, champagne flutes, cut-glass tumblers . . . Keep them all together if you can, to take one more stress out of hosting. Be ready to issue instructions when someone asks what they can do to help: 'Oh, yes, please could you get the cake-stand out of the cupboard, the one we use just this one day each year, but it would cause a mutiny if we served the bûche de Noël on anything different . . .'

Christmas music, books and films

These might be kits you keep digitally, festive playlists on your favourite streaming platforms. Or, like me, you might have a couple of Christmas tote-bags stuffed with carol books and story books given to your parents when they were children, a festive library added to by each new generation; CDs and DVDs that have been played every year since you can remember. Christmas entertainment begins in our house with *The Nightmare Before Christmas* on Hallowe'en, and Nigel Slater's *The Christmas Chronicles* are my evening treat when the rest of the house is tucked up in bed and I feel like indulging in some fantasy festive days.

Christmas stockings

One year I asked for posh Hunter wellies for Christmas. They came in a posh Hunter wellies box with handy carrying handle. Perfect for keeping the Christmas stockings in! (Could also be kept with the wrapping kit.)

Christmas-tree kit

- ☆ Tree-stand
- ☆ Fairy lights (you'll thank yourself for taking the time to store them untangled. We use the old boxes from baking parchment and tinfoil: wrap the lights round the cardboard roll and the box helps keep everything together. Wrapping-paper rolls also work. And make sure you keep the plug/converter box thing in the same place – attach it with some of those millions of rubber bands you don't know what to do with).
- ☆ Tinsel, baubles and decorations
- ☆ Star/fairy/tree topper of your choice

☆ Tree skirt (my mother made ours from a big circle of thick red felt with a sparkly gold-ribbon border, and I treasure it)

Craft kit

Do you love making things? Know some kids who do?

☆ Glitter (biodegradable), stickers (ditto), tissue paper, stapler
☆ Non-toxic paper glue (hot-glue gun if age-appropriate)
☆ Old scraps of wrapping paper and last year's Christmas cards

Stationery, sewing, knitting and craft kits and supplies, stamps and ink pads, wax-seal kits, fancy writing paper and notecards . . . all make lovely Christmas presents. If you're the lucky recipient, store them away for next year or, if you know you'll probably never get round to using them, pass them on via your local charity shop, and give someone else the pleasure.

DIY kit

Repainting the house, hanging new curtains and redecorating are all traditional around this time of year – in the warmer climates at least. While it's nice to have everything shiny and new, you may not feel like adding a major DIY project to your Christmas timeline (and I really don't recommend starting to wallpaper the downstairs toilet the day before the in-laws are due to descend, however much this is the only chance you've had all year to get round to it). But it's definitely worth having some basic SOS items to hand – there will be at least one year when the pipes burst and you can't find an emergency plumber for love nor money. Check that you know where your stopcocks are!

- ☆ Hammer, pliers, adjustable spanner
- ☆ Screwdriver with changeable heads
- ☆ Selection of: nails, screws, picture hooks, cup hooks
- ☆ Plunger
- ☆ Wood glue, superglue

Electrical essentials

Okay, they're not essential, and it would be good for the world if we didn't see them as consumables/disposable, and we must definitely recycle them responsibly. But bearing the environmental consequences in mind, it is extremely helpful to have:

- ☆ Rechargeable batteries, device chargers, speakers, extension cables, lightbulbs
- ☆ Headphones (noise-cancelling if possible; this could be your only way of getting some peace and quiet)

Scissors

The one thing you can guarantee with scissors is you can never find them when you need them. So, the trick is to have many, many pairs. At least one in each kit, and a few for luck. A good pair of scissors can also make a surprisingly lovely and even beautiful gift that you might not buy for yourself.

Tape

Like scissors, you can never have enough. Try to find eco/biodegradable tape if you can. Brown parcel tape, sellotape, matte scotch tape, masking tape, washi tape, fancy festive tape. Posh tapes make great stocking fillers, too.

Washing-up kit

Essential: no excuses for anyone not to do their bit!

Wrapping kit

- ☆ Tape, ribbon/string, scissors
- ☆ Gift tags (cut up last year's cards and use the fronts: a hole punch is handy for this)
- ☆ Paper/tissue paper/gift bags/*furoshiki* cloth

Wreath-making kit

Perhaps you have a wreath you keep in your Advent kit. If you fancy making your own, you'll need:

- ☆ Wreath base – you can buy them, or make your own from woven willow or an old wire coat hanger
- ☆ Florist wire and wire cutters/scissors you don't mind getting blunt
- ☆ Garden twine
- ☆ Pruning shears
- ☆ Cinnamon sticks, dried citrus slices, pine cones, eucalyptus leaves, etc.
- ☆ Ribbon
- ☆ Fresh moss, greenery, flowers, berries, whatever catches your eye this year

I

Over the green and yellow rice fields sweep the shadows of the autumn clouds, followed by the swift-chasing sun.
The bees forget to sip their honey; drunken with the light they foolishly hum and hover; and the ducks in the sandy riverbank clamour in joy for mere nothing.
None shall go back home, brothers, this morning, none shall go to work.
We will take the blue sky by storm and plunder the space as we run.
Laughters fly floating in the air like foams in the flood.
Brothers, we shall squander our morning in futile songs.

II

Keep me fully glad with nothing. Only take my hand in your hand.
In the gloom of the deepening night take up my heart and play with it as you list. Bind me close to you with nothing.
I will spread myself out at your feet and lie still. Under this clouded sky I will meet silence with silence. I will become one with the night clasping the earth in my breast.
Make my life glad with nothing.
The rains sweep the sky from end to end. Jasmines in the wet untameable wind revel in their own perfume. The cloud-hidden stars thrill in secret. Let me fill to the full of my heart with nothing but my own depth of joy.

III

My soul is alight with your infinitude of stars.
Your world has broken upon me like a flood.
The flowers of your garden blossom in my body.
The joy of life that is everywhere burns like an incense in
    my heart.
And the breath of all things plays on my life as on a pipe
    of reeds.

Rabindra Nath Tagore | 'Poems' *from* 'The Gardener'

September's

— Special Days —

Season of mists and mellow fruitfulness,
    Close bosom-friend of the maturing sun;
Conspiring with him how to load and bless
    With fruit the vines that round the thatch-eves run;
To bend with apples the moss'd cottage-trees,
    And fill all fruit with ripeness to the core;
        To swell the gourd, and plump the hazel shells
    With a sweet kernel; to set budding more,
And still more, later flowers for the bees,
Until they think warm days will never cease,
        For summer has o'er-brimm'd their clammy cells.

John Keats | *from* 'To Autumn'

21/22/23

September

Equinox
('Equal Night')

There's a shift in the air that comes with the equinox – a sense of anticipation that stirs and builds.

In the Northern and Southern Tropics of Cancer and Capricorn, it brings physical changes to the natural world: the weather, the behaviour of plants and animals.

The sun rises between the fifth and sixth towers of the Chankillo Solar Observatory in the Peruvian desert, bringing spring to the Southern Hemisphere; and solstice celebrations at Stonehenge greet the first light of autumn in the North.

It signals the time for planting, or harvest.

For emerging or retreating.

And this is when we begin to feel the first tingles of excitement for the festive times ahead . . .

Spring Equinox in the Southern Hemisphere

~ OSTARA ~

Celebration of life, fertility and the end of winter.

Flowers, trees and animals are waking from their slumber . . .

Collect wild flowers and make flower chains | decorate eggs | go bilby-spotting | frolic with lambs | make honey cakes | dress and decorate in the colours of the season: red, green, pale purple, yellow, pink | feast your eyes on daffodils and bluebells, violets and marigolds, golden wattle blooms | tuck a jacaranda flower behind your ear | breathe in the scent of jasmine | brew hibiscus syrup | gather herbs: borage, marjoram, lemon myrtle | start something new | nurture your seedlings | soak in the energy of life bursting out all around | watch blossom swirl and dance like snowflakes

Meditate on new beginnings.

Find what is lost.

Autumn Equinox in the Northern Hemisphere

~ MABON ~

A feast of thanksgiving to celebrate earth's bounty.

It's the end of the summer harvest. The monsoon season is coming to a close.

Birds fly south to seek a warmer home . . .

Go scrumping | eat apple pie | fill a cornucopia with fruits of the fall | gather acorns and rosehips | find a marigold | hold a pomegranate | plant flower bulbs | make a corn doll | curl up with a book | snuggle under a soft blanket | treat yourself to early nights and long lie-ins . . .

Enjoy the simple pleasures.

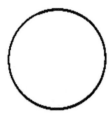

Look for the Harvest Moon, the full moon closest to the equinox, which marks the day of Harvest Festival in the West and the Moon Festival in the East.

It's the biggest, brightest full moon of the year, and often seems to shine with a golden glow.

Celebrate the safe gathering of the harvest with corn dolls and mead.

Honour those older and wiser than you.

Find the highest point nearby and walk there, to gaze at the moon.

Though far apart,
share the beauty of the moon together.

Su Shi | *from* 'Water-Accent Song'

21

September

International Day of Peace

Let us construct a fort of peace in each
individual's mind . . . and let us make peace
as the motto of mankind . . .
Let us wish for a world as one family.

Chiyoji Nakagawa, creator of the UN Peace Bell

~

Twice a year, the Japanese Peace Bell is tolled at the United Nations: at the vernal equinox, in celebration of the annual Earth Day, and on every opening of the General Assembly in September, for the International Day of Peace.

It is a Buddhist Temple Bell, cast from sword guards, bullets and coins donated by 65 nations around the world.

On its side are eight Japanese characters that say, 'Long live absolute world peace.'

22/23
September

The sun enters kind, intelligent

~ LIBRA ~

Find balance and harmony
through others and through art.

. . .

Month of the

~ DOG ~

Brave, loyal, clever, lively.

29

September

Michaelmas Day

The date of new beginnings.

Michaelmas daisies* bloom, their star-like flowers scattering bright colour: purple for wisdom, white for innocence, red for devotion and pink for love.

St Michael the Archangel brings protection and prosperity.

Angel of Mercy, the Angel Mika'il, is a friend to humanity and giver of rain and food.

* also known as asters, or starwort

Let me remember you, voices of little insects,
Weeds in the moonlight, fields that are tangled with asters,
Let me remember, soon will the winter be on us,
Snow-hushed and heavy.

Sara Teasdale | *from* 'September Midnight'

30

September

Month of the Ivy begins in the Celtic Tree Calendar

Strength ~ determination

A time to banish negativity.

It was thought that wearing a crown of ivy would stave off a hangover – or bring inspiration to poets.

Its long tendrils of heart-shaped leaves and starbursts of green-black berries bring peace and protection from evil to the home.

Listen for the buzzing of the ivy bees as they feast on its pollen.

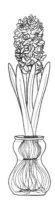

If you are green-fingered, here is a little reminder that hyacinths planted now will flower in 10–12 weeks . . .

Choose 'prepared' bulbs and find a jar or vase with a neck just wide enough to hold a bulb. Fill with water until the jar is three-quarters full and balance the bulb pointed-end upwards, its rounded base a centimetre or two above the surface.

Tuck your jar somewhere cool and dark where it won't be disturbed (or nibbled by mice!).

Check in on it and give it fresh water each week.

Watch as the roots reach down and shoots begin to appear; and all going well, they'll be blooming in time to brighten your windowsills with a promise of spring for Christmas!

Serenely sweet you gild the silent grove,
My friend, my goddess, and my guide.

Lady Mary Wortley Montagu | *from* 'A Hymn to the Moon'

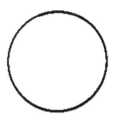

September / October

– Festivals –

that move with the Moon

Some of the special days we celebrate change dates each year, because they follow the cycles of the moon.

Here are some of the festivals that usually occur around mid-September to mid-October. Check this year's calendar to find out exactly when . . .

All day I have watched the purple vine leaves
Fall into the water.
And now in the moonlight they still fall,
But each leaf is fringed with silver.

Amy Lowell | 'Autumn'

Many people believe that the phases of the moon affect our mood, personalities, outlooks and our lives – whether we are aware of it or not. Perhaps it tugs at the water within us, much as it pulls at the tides . . .

 New Moon | Waxing Crescent
~ Send your hopes & desires out into the world ~

 First Quarter | Waxing Gibbous
~ Nurture your life ~

 Full Moon | Waning Gibbous
~ Introspect & be grateful ~

 Last Quarter | Waning Crescent
~ Compose & rest ~

Months in the Islamic Hijri calendar follow a lunar cycle – meaning that the holy month of Ramadan moves back by ten or eleven days in the Gregorian calendar each year. The precise day of Eid-al Fitr, 'The Feast of the Breaking of the Fast' that comes at the end of Ramadan, is only known at the sighting of the new crescent moon.

Isn't there something so powerful in the feeling that millions of people all over the world are watching for the moon, waiting and celebrating together?

New Moon

The new moon is considered to be a time of great power.

A day of still, dark quiet; a time to tidy, to process and release.

Draw on the accommodating energy of **Libra**.
Seek imbalances and set them straight.
Make peace.
Find closure.
Create tranquillity, harmony, beauty.

Eat simple foods – milk, water, fruit and nuts, soup.

Light a candle at sunset.

Set intentions.
With the new moon: to find ways to establish lost balance.
With the full moon: to seek equality in your partnerships.

Let go of old and tired things, make space for new and exciting beginnings.

What are you carrying in your sack this month?

Understanding the cycles of the moon is a good reminder that we have phases of energy and productivity, and all of us need time to stop and rest every so often.

It's especially important in these months before Christmas, when the pressures can just seem to build and build.

Santa's sack might be big enough to carry presents for every child in the world; but unlike Grandfather Frost we're not magical beings, and we can't carry it all.

The still dark nights around the new moon each month are a good prompt to have a look at everything we've gathered and to decide: what to keep? What could we discard, or put aside for later, another time, next year?

Set down the sack of your Christmas expectations, have a look at what's inside, and pick out the things that are special and important just for you.

That's what Santa's gift is, after all: he doesn't leave you the whole sack; he knows just what you need – a stocking's worth of delights, and no more.

~ Navratri, Autumn Nine Nights Festival ~

Festivals with their roots in the Indian sub-continent follow a lunar calendar, so it's the phases of the moon that determine their dates.

The new moon around this time brings Navratri – the nine-night festival honouring the divine feminine, through the nine forms of the goddess Durga.

1. Maa Shailputri, daughter of the mountains
2. Brahmacharini, embodiment of perseverance and penance
3. Matachandraghanta, who brings courage and protection from evil
4. Kushmanda, the 'smiling goddess' who disperses darkness and grants wealth and health
5. Skandamata, who graces with prosperity and power
6. Katyayani, the 'warrior goddess'
7. Kalaratri, the fiercest and most ferocious form of the goddess
8. Mahagauri, who brings fulfilment of desires and relief from suffering
9. Siddhidatri, giver of knowledge

Dussehra, the 'defeat of the ten-headed demon' festival, falls on the tenth day, and is a celebration of the femininity which protects and sustains life on earth.

Dress, accessorise or decorate in the colour of the day – allocated and announced each year. Check the local media to find out what to wear!

Orange ~ brightness, happiness, positive energy

White ~ purity, innocence, inner peace & security

Red ~ passion & love, fearlessness, vigour & vitality

Royal blue ~ power, panache, elegance, richness & tranquillity

Yellow ~ optimism & joy

Green ~ growth, fertility, serenity, tranquillity, new beginnings

Grey ~ balanced emotions, zeal & determination to destroy evil

Purple ~ luxury, grandeur, nobility, opulence & richness, ambition & power

Peacock blue-green ~ compassion, freshness, uniqueness, individuality

Pink ~ hope, self-refinement, social upliftment

~

A time for family reunions, exchange of gifts and blessings.

~Rosh Hashanah ~

A blessing of the new moon is recited at the beginning of each Jewish month.

Tishrei, 'beginning', is the first month of the civil year, and the seventh month of the ecclesiastical year. Rosh Hashanah, 'The Head of the Year', is celebrated with the blasting of a hollow ram's horn on the first day of Tishrei. It's the traditional anniversary of the creation of Adam and Eve, and begins a cycle of commemorative days filled with ritual, reflection and joyful celebrations.

1–2 Rosh Hashanah 'Head of the Year'
Eat apples dipped in honey to sweeten the year ahead.

1 Creation of Adam & Eve

10 Yom Kippur
It is traditional to make a donation to charity, to mark the day of atonement.

15–21 Sukkot
During the seven-day Harvest Festival, 'four kinds' are bound together in a lulav bundle to symbolise unity between different types of people: a palm branch, two willows, three myrtles and a citron lemon.

When the first dark had fallen around them
And the leaves were weary of praise,
In the clear silence Beauty found them
And shewed them all her ways.

In the high noon of the heavenly garden
Where the angels sunned with the birds,
Beauty, before their hearts could harden,
Had taught them heavenly words.

When they fled in the burning weather
And nothing dawned but a dream,
Beauty fasted their hands together
And cooled them at her stream.

And when day wearied and night grew stronger,
And they slept as the beautiful must,
Then she bided a little longer,
And blossomed from their dust.

Marjorie Pickthall | 'Adam and Eve'

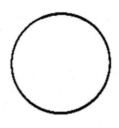

Full Corn Moon

Barley Moon

Wine Moon

Song Moon

Child Moon

Falling Leaves Moon

Leaves Turning Moon

Mating Moon

Moon of Brown Leaves

Rutting Moon

Moon When the Rice is Laid up to Dry

Yellow Leaf Moon

~

Abundance ~ Sharing ~ Transformation

~ Valmiki Jayanti ~

This full moon day is Valmiki Jayanti, celebrating the first poet of the Sanskrit language. The actual date of his birth anniversary is not known, but it's said that this legendary teacher of Rama and Sita's children had a face which glowed like the full moon . . .

> On the gay and bright pavilion, on the high and shady trees,
> Banners rose and glittering streamers, flags that fluttered in the breeze!
> Actors gay and nimble dancers, singers skilled in lightsome song,
> With their antics and their music pleased the gay and gathered throng
> . . .
>
> Women wore the scented garland, merry maids the censer lit,
> Men with broom and sprinkled water swept the spacious mart and street,
> Rows of trees and posts they planted hung with lamps for coming night,
> That the midnight dark might rival splendour of the noonday light

Valmiki | *from* 'The Ramayana'

~ Sharad Purnima ~

Each full moon – or Purnima – is observed as a special day in the Hindu lunar calendar.

Sharad Purnima this month brings the end of the monsoon season and the beginning of winter.

Take a long bath, or a morning swim.

Fill a silver bowl with kheer rice pudding, infused in milk with cardamom.

Leave it overnight in moonlight, to catch the divine nectar of the moon.

~ Pavarana ~

In Buddhism, the full moon – especially the bright full moon of autumn – is a symbol of truth and enlightenment. Each lunar month begins with a full moon festival, and the October full moon heralds a 'month of light' at the end of the rainy season.

The Pavarana ceremony of repentance and pardoning marks the end of the three lunar months of Buddhist Vassa ('rains retreat').

Pay thanks to parents, teachers, anyone who has helped you through difficulty; and receive blessings and loving kindness in turn.

Seek out lotus flowers – flower of this month – rising from muddy water as a sacred symbol of beauty and purity.

~ Double Ninth Festival ~
Chrysanthemum Day

The ninth day of the ninth month in the Chinese lunar calendar is particularly auspicious. Both day and month are yang characters, and nine is the largest number, reflecting a long, healthy life.

Long ago, it was a day to drive away danger; now it is a time for honouring ancestors, flying kites, climbing mountains and making flower cakes to eat with chrysanthemum tea and wine – while reciting or learning poems about chrysanthemums!

Originally a wild daisy, chrysanthemums have been cultivated in Chinese gardens for thousands of years, prized for their hardy flowers that grow even in frost. Along with bamboo, plum and orchid, it is considered one of the four 'noble plants'. Chrysanthemum wine is said to clear the vision and refresh the mind.

Introduced to Japan by Zen monks in the 5th century, the chrysanthemum seal is the symbol of the Japanese emperor, representing longevity, rejuvenation and nobility. Red flowers are given to loved and respected people.

The botanical name for chrysanthemum means 'golden flower' and although white chrysanthemums are traditionally seen as a grave flower (especially in Italy) they can also conjure meanings of holiness and blessedness. In southern Germany, white chrysanthemums are brought into homes on Christmas Eve, symbolising the Christ Child.

Fourth-century poet Tao Chien famously turned down a top-level government job in favour of retiring to his chrysanthemum garden to drink wine with his friends.

> I pluck chrysanthemums from the East hedge
> And, leisurely, look to the mountains in the South.
> The air there is beautiful day and night.
> Birds fly, returning together.
> There is clear meaning to this –
> I wish I could find the words.

Tao Chien | *from* 'Drinking Wine'

It's hard not to notice nature in October – she's bursting out all over the place. Bright-green acorns thunder down from the oak tree in our garden, to be caught up by squirrels busily hoarding for the days when the branches are bare; and birds noisily announce their holiday plans as they head off on migration.

The hedgerows are full of treasures:
rosehip baubles and soft-furred golden quince,
star-bursts of teasels and fluffy tufts of old man's beard –
nature is already decking the halls, preparing for
the party days to come.

October was a beautiful month at Green Gables, when the birches in the hollow turned as golden as sunshine and the maples behind the orchard were royal crimson and the wild cherry trees along the lane put on the loveliest shades of dark red and bronzy green, while the fields sunned themselves in aftermaths.

Anne revelled in the world of colour about her.

'Oh, Marilla,' she exclaimed one Saturday morning, coming dancing in with her arms full of gorgeous boughs, 'I'm so glad I live in a world where there are Octobers. It would be terrible if we just skipped from September to November, wouldn't it? Look at these maple branches. Don't they give you a thrill – several thrills? I'm going to decorate my room with them . . . One can dream so much better in a room where there are pretty things.'

L. M. Montgomery | *from* Anne of Green Gables

IT'S harvest time for bounty everywhere – fruit to be made into jams and jellies, vegetables to be pickled or simmered into rich chutneys, and one memorable year, great bins filled with apple juice fermenting into potent cloudy cider.

At first frost, it's time to head up the lane for sloe-picking in the hedgerows: the wild bushes of the blackthorn like something from a fairy tale, sprung overnight to protect a sleeping princess. Reaching past the dagger-like thorns to harvest the solitary round berries is a labour of love: a long afternoon in crisp bright sunshine to gather just enough for a gin bottle's worth . . . And then the long wait until the magic brew of sugar and booze is ready to drink.

Mother Christmas fills cool dark cupboards with jewel-like jars of sweet things brewing and maturing for just the right number of weeks until they are ready to make the perfect gift. And when that's done, out comes the sewing machine, to stitch costumes and party clothes and special bows, lovely hand-crafted things to be sold at the Christmas fayre.

The Elves have their Christmas lists: who gets cards and presents, and the shopping has begun.

Rehearsals start in earnest for festive shows and concerts. Deadlines are in place for anyone who has Christmas as their peak time for making or selling or hospitality-ing.

The serious business of Christmas begins . . .

~ Christmas Cooking ~
Preparing for your Favourite Feasts

I really like cooking. As long as there's no room full of hangry people waiting on the results and demanding snacks because the food's running late so you get distracted assembling canapés because it's Christmas and you feel bad just chucking them a bag of crisps.

I like to experiment with flavours and cook with what I have or what caught my eye in the greengrocer's that day. I really, really don't like to plan ahead and remember what to buy in advance, so I feel the pressure of the shops being shut for twenty-four hours when I'm so used to being able to pop to the corner if I run out of milk or I forgot to get the loo roll.

But that's the thing, isn't it? It's only twenty-four hours. We can probably survive. Or give ourselves a break and do it two days later when all the ridiculous prices have suddenly dropped so the supermarkets can clear their shelves of sprouts and socks'n'stilton gift packs.

I find myself muttering the mantra, 'It's only a Sunday roast. I can do a Sunday roast' and angsting over whether it's okay not to have turkey or Christmas pudding when no one likes turkey or Christmas pudding, but then what makes it a Christmas dinner and not just a Sunday roast?

Let's remember that for some people the real treat is being allowed to eat chocolate for breakfast and fish fingers with just roasties, no greens, because that's their favourite and they really hate sprouts. And maybe this year I'll just cook what I like to cook . . .

Stocking up the freezer

Perhaps you are like the lady in front of me in the butcher's queue one October, who announced that she'd bought a new freezer specially to hold the turkey and wanted to get her order in now . . . Or perhaps you're like me and the very idea fills you with fear because you might forget to take it out and it would never defrost in time . . . adding a whole new layer of anxiety in the will-the-turkey-ever-be-ready-to-eat-before-midnight scenario.

If you do have the freezer space (if not an actual dedicated outbuilding) then there are a couple of things you might add to your weekly shop to get ahead of the Christmas frenzy that can leave the shelves bare of vital items you don't give a second thought to most of the year.

- ☆ Frozen cranberries, cherries, raspberries and strawberries are great for making jewel-red sauces and compotes
- ☆ Peas – you probably already have them but surely as essential as toilet roll!
- ☆ Frozen spinach for that lovely dark evergreen
- ☆ Frozen edamame beans can be harder to find but are a great way to add a pop of fresh green to the table if you do
- ☆ Other veg like sprouts are less successful frozen, which is a shame because then someone else would've done that fiddly prep stuff for you
- ☆ Margarita pizzas – think of them as your safety net. Ready in fifteen minutes for fussy eaters, or if you forgot to take the turkey out of the freezer in time.
- ☆ If you eat them, then streaky bacon, smoked salmon, pigs in blankets, stuffing, gammon ham ready for boiling and baking, turkey mince and turkey fillets are all things that freeze well, defrost relatively quickly and can be used to

rustle up quick bung-in-the-oven or pop-it-on-a-doily Christmassy treats. Likewise, nut roasts and veggie sausages, mince pies and mouth-sized pastry morsels.

☆ And Mother Christmas always has pots of stock and warming soup and tempting pâtés ready to be defrosted in a trice for unexpected guests. Use silicon muffin trays or old yoghurt pots if you're freezing your own and you'll have handy portions at the ready.

☆ Keep a canny eye out for discounted bread at the end of the day, or freeze any leftover bread instead of throwing it out when it gets stale – it's great for breadcrumbs and bread sauce, or baking thinly sliced Melba toast for your pâté and salmon. Or just freeze it in slices for toast when you've run out and the shops are shut.

Kitting out the kitchen

Wouldn't it be lovely to have everything beautifully arrayed and right there where you need it, like the TV chefs do? Take a quick audit of your kitchen set-up: what could you do to make it a real pleasure to work in this space?

Have you got room for a pot or two of fresh herbs? I have to put mine on the windowsill so I remember to water them when I wash up.

What's your spice collection like? Every so often I get all Home Makeover and put them in alphabetical order, but it never lasts long. I love my higgledy-piggledy drawers with the eclectic mix of packets and jars, although I always have massive envy for people with beautiful colour-graduated fragrant displays.

Stock up the store cupboards with key ingredients you know you'll need: flour and oils, beans and pulses, garlic and tomato purée, cocoa powder, good dark chocolate and packets of jelly, sugars and syrups, sponge fingers and coffee, tortillas and tacos, ketchup and mayo, your favourite sweet and salty sauces, honey and jams, chutneys and pickles, rice and pasta, couscous and quinoa, nuts and dried fruit, capers, sardines and anchovies . . . The trick is to know you have the things you like to cook with, and then even if you don't make up your mind what you're going to cook until you find out how you feel on the day, you've got plenty of choice.

Also remember baking parchment for lining cake tins and baking trays for gingerbread and pavlova; and tinfoil for wrapping turkey and nut roast and leftovers.

Storage boxes

Mother Christmas filled Christmas tins with treats: shortbread and chocolate fudge cake, flapjacks and mince pies with pastry so fine and buttery it was almost caramelised. A grand glass dome covered the Christmas cake, and there were smaller domes to protect the cheese.

I'm a fan of glass storage containers myself. I don't have room for beautiful glass domes, and I like things that stack and show what's inside – especially if what's inside are star-shaped gingerbreads and toasted nuts and chocolate cake dusted in icing sugar.

Hold on to any takeaway containers you have, they're going to be super useful for leftovers and freezing things.

Selective eaters, preferences, intolerances and allergies

Find out as soon as possible what dietary requirements you need to cater for, especially if there are any different requirements from what you're used to accommodating. If you're catering a party, include at least one thing that a vegan allergic to nuts could eat. In my experience, children can be unbelievably pedantic about their food (yes, I eat ham but not that type of ham) so it's okay to ask their parents/responsible adults to bring something that will be accepted and save everyone the pain. And always serve something delicious and non-alcoholic to drink.

~ What tastes like Christmas to you? ~

Christmas food is national, regional, seasonal, personal. Your big feast might be at Thanksgiving, or Christmas Eve, New Year or Epiphany. You might fast during Advent, or on Christmas Eve. You might dine on fish, or beef, or perhaps have a fusion of different food cultures woven into your family heritage. Maybe you eat the same things each year, maybe you like to try something new. You'll definitely have favourites and dishes that bring back memories with every bite.

The three core tastes

When you're putting dishes together, the secret is getting the balance between these three. They're also shortcuts to making something simple but impressive. Whether layered together or served alongside each other, the perfect mouthful of a canapé or a full dish to delight, there's a special magic in this combination . . .

Creamy ~ Cream, cream cheese, mascarpone, yoghurt, tahini. Spread or blend, stir through with fruit fresh or compote, vegetables grated or gently sautéed, a zesty squirt of citrus, a swirl of melted chocolate, layer with cake drenched in coffee or fruit juice or booze. Make dips, spreads and puddings – and the best bit is always the last lick of the bowl!

Salty ~ Cheese, fish, cured meats, salted butter, roasted nuts. A tangy slice, the crunchy base, a pinch, a handful; always in moderation, to add the perfect kick.

Sweet ~ Fruit fresh, dried and candied, sprinkles and syrups, pickles and compotes, jellies and jams. That something extra to elevate the savoury, a treat to pop in your mouth or a show-stopping spectacular to round off the meal.

The essential ingredients

These, for me, are the flavours of Christmas:

Almonds ~ Sugared, toasted, the scented secret of marzipan.

Bay ~ For infusing milk and rice puddings, adding a touch of evergreen.

Brandy ~ For drenching the cake, blending with sugary butter – or setting the pudding ablaze (also sometimes the holly sprig!)

Candied peel ~ Chopped in fruit cakes, figgy pudding and mince pies – or left in long strips, coated in crystals of sugar or dipped in shiny dark chocolate that cracks to the bite.

Cheese ~ A melted Camembert centrepiece, a festive fondue, an enticing board with all your favourites – just don't forget the crackers and a bunch of purple grapes . . .

Chocolate orange ~ The crinkly weight of it in the toe of a stocking. One smart tap, a segment for all. Fight for that little chocolate navel at its heart!

Cranberries ~ Rich bittersweet sauce served hot on the side; save enough to have cold with leftovers. Or brewed into cordial, simmered with sugar and lemon juice and perhaps a little cinnamon, infused, cooled and strained and served with bubbles of soda water or tonic and a bright slice of orange.

Dates ~ Shiny as beetles under a crinkling cellophane carapace, nestled beside their own special prong. Chopped into breakfast granola, stirred through fruit salad, dotted deep in the heart of cakes and puddings. Rich, dark date syrup, the perfect companion to Christmas spices.

Fresh fruits ~ Ruby grapefruit, blood oranges, lychees, quinces, sloes, pears. Bowls piled with clementines, little handfuls of sunshine.

Poached, or sliced and scattered. Chopped into a Christmas fruit salad, served with spiced granola. My father's 'magic orange', with the peel carefully sliced and pulled out into petals, like a lotus flower.

Gingerbread ~ Houses and the crisp snap of biscuits.

Mince pies ~ Sweet, these days, though still named for their savoury ancestor. The first mince pie is the first taste of Christmas. Rich butter pastry, an oozing heart of cooked chopped fruit and secret suet sweetened with juice and brown sugar and that unique mix of spices that has Christmas in every bite.

Apparently, if you eat a mince pie on each of the twelve days of Christmas, you'll have twelve days of happiness!

Mulled cider/apple juice ~ A lighter/non-alcoholic alternative to mulled wine, perfect for nights by the bonfire or out singing carols. Infused with cinnamon and cloves, apples and oranges sliced in star-centred circles, adorned with star anise. Mulled wine/glug/glühwein are also traditional, of course; my best ever was from a paper cup, with the rim dipped in crystals of demerara sugar – a sweet and spicy, sticky handwarmer for a magical procession of lights.

Panettone ~ I can never resist the beautiful tins with slippery cord handles. That brown and gold paper that doesn't quite peel away from the bottom. An essential ingredient of Christmas French toast or bread and butter pudding.

Pavlova ~ Melting mountains of meringue with towering peaks of whipped cream, topped by jewels of seasonal fruit or enticing pools of fruit compote.

Red cabbage ~ Cooked slow and spiced, or grated into slaw.

Sage ~ With onion for stuffing.

Spices ~ The secret ingredient: a pinch of spice in your cooking, essential oils, scented candles – one sniff and it's Christmas!

Fragrant scrolls of cinnamon tied with ribbon or bobbing alongside star anise when mulling wine. Cloves studded into oranges, floating with bay leaves in milk for bread sauce, finely ground with ginger and allspice in cakes and biscuits. Vanilla-speckled ice cream. Nutmeg grated on top of hot chocolate, rice pudding or creamy cocktails.

Sprouts ~ Fairy cabbages, marked with a cross. Lightly steamed, emerald green and crunchy; or grated for a Christmas coleslaw; or quickly stir-fried with salty bacon, pine nuts and a sprinkling of ground cinnamon.

Sugar ~ Dust everything with icing sugar!

Dark sugars and syrups bring decadent richness to everything they touch.

Trifle ~ My sister's favourite! Served in a cut-glass bowl to showcase all those delicious layers of cream, extra rich custard, ruby-red fruit, sherry-soaked sponge cake.

Walnuts ~ A bowl of little brains to crack yourself.

The sun burns hotly thro' the gums
As down the road old Rogan comes –
   The hatter from the lonely hut
   Beside the track to Woollybutt.
      He likes to spend his Christmas with us here.

. . .

   'It ain't a day for workin' hard.'
Says Dad. 'One day a year don't matter much.'
And then dishevelled, hot and red,
Mum, thro' the doorway puts her head
   And says, 'This Christmas cooking, My!
   The sun's near fit for cooking by.'

. . .

'Your fault,' says Dad, 'you know it is.
Plum puddin'! on a day like this,
   And roasted turkeys! Spare me days,
   I can't get over women's ways.
      In climates such as this the thing's all wrong.
A bit of cold corned beef an' bread
Would do us very well instead.'

. . .

The dinner's served – full bite and sup.
'Come on,' says Mum, 'Now all sit up.'
   The meal takes on a festive air;
   And even father eats his share
      And passes up his plate to have some more.
He laughs and says it's Christmas time,
'That's cookin', Mum. The stuffin's prime.'

. . .

Then, with his black pipe well alight,
Old Rogan brings the kids delight
   By telling o'er again his yarns
    Of Christmas tide 'mid English barns
     When he was, long ago, a farmer's boy.
His old eyes glisten as he sees
Half glimpses of old memories,
   Of whitened fields and winter snows,
    And yuletide logs and mistletoes,
     And all that half-forgotten, hallowed joy.

The children listen, mouths agape,
And see a land with no escape
   Fro biting cold and snow and frost -
    A land to all earth's brightness lost,
     A strange and freakish Christmas land to them.
...

The sun slants redly thro' the gums
As quietly the evening comes,
   And Rogan gets his old grey mare,
    That matches well his own grey hair,
     And rides away into the setting sun.
'Ah, well,' says Dad. 'I got to say
I never spent a lazier day.
   We ought to get that top fence wired.'
    'My!' sighs poor Mum. 'But I am tired!
     An' all that washing up still to be done.'

C. J. Dennis | *from* 'A Bush Christmas'

October's

— Special Days —

Second Saturday of October

~ World Migratory Bird Day ~

Every year, entire populations of birds make miraculous journeys between breeding grounds and overwintering territories separated by thousands of kilometres.

Their flight paths cross war zones and disputed territories, relying on air currents and natural phenomena buffeted and threatened by climate change.

Go bird-spotting today and wonder where any gathering flocks you see might be headed. Wish them well on their travels.

October gave a party;
The leaves by hundreds came—
The Chestnuts, Oaks, and Maples,
And leaves of every name.
The Sunshine spread a carpet,
And everything was grand,
Miss Weather led the dancing,
Professor Wind the band.

The Chestnuts came in yellow,
The Oaks in crimson dressed;
The lovely Misses Maple
In scarlet looked their best;
All balanced to their partners,
And gaily fluttered by;
The sight was like a rainbow
New fallen from the sky.

George Cooper | *from* 'October's Party'

~ Black History Month ~

Come when the nights are bright with stars
Or come when the moon is mellow;
Come when the sun his golden bars
Drops on the hay-field yellow.
Come in the twilight soft and gray,
Come in the night or come in the day,
Come, O love, whene'er you may,
And you are welcome, welcome.

You are sweet, O Love, dear Love,
You are soft as the nesting dove.
Come to my heart and bring it to rest
As the bird flies home to its welcome nest.

Come when my heart is full of grief
Or when my heart is merry;
Come with the falling of the leaf
Or with the redd'ning cherry.
Come when the year's first blossom blows,
Come when the summer gleams and glows,
Come with the winter's drifting snows,
And you are welcome, welcome.

Paul Laurence Dunbar | 'Invitation to Love'

~ World Mental Health Month ~

The rustling of leaves under the feet in woods and under hedges;
The crumpling of cat-ice and snow down wood-rides, narrow lanes, and every street causeway;
Rustling through a wood or rather rushing, while the wind halloos in the oak-toop like thunder;
The rustle of birds' wings startled from their nests or flying unseen into the bushes;
The whizzing of larger birds overhead in a wood, such as crows, puddocks, buzzards;
The trample of robins and woodlarks on the brown leaves, and the patter of squirrels on the green moss;
The fall of an acorn on the ground, the pattering of nuts on the hazel branches as they fall from ripeness;
The flirt of the groundlark's wing from the stubbles – how sweet such pictures on dewy mornings, when the dew flashes from its brown feathers.

John Clare | 'Pleasant Sounds'

2
October

**Mahatma Gandhi's birthday
International Day of Non-Violence**

I offer you peace
I offer you love
I offer you friendship
I see your beauty
I hear your need
I feel your feelings
My wisdom flows from the highest source
I salute that source in you
Let us work together
For unity and peace.

M. K. Gandhi (attributed) | 'Prayer for Peace'

4

October

Feast of St Francis

Where there is hatred, let me sow love;
Where there is injury, pardon;
Where there is error, the truth;
Where there is doubt, the faith;
Where there is despair, hope;
Where there is darkness, light;
And where there is sadness, joy.

St Francis of Assisi (attributed) | *from* 'Prayer of St Francis'

5

October

World Teachers' Day

They carried Mrs. Nipson a large slice of cake, and a basket full of the beautiful red apples. All the teachers were remembered.

. . .

Last of all, Katy made a choice little selection from her stores, a splendid apple, a couple of fine pears, and a handful of raisins and figs, and, with a few of the freshest flowers in a wine-glass, she went down the Row and tapped at Miss Jane's door.

Miss Jane was sitting up for the first time, wrapped in a shawl, and looking very thin and pale. Katy, who had almost ceased to be afraid of her, went in cheerily.

'We've had a delicious box from home, Miss Jane, full of all sorts of things. It has been such fun unpacking it! I've brought you an apple, some pears, and this little bunch of flowers. Wasn't it a nice Christmas for us?'

'Yes,' said Miss Jane, 'very nice indeed. I heard some one saying in the entry that you had a box. Thank you,' as Katy set the basket and glass on the table. 'Those flowers are very sweet. I wish you a Merry Christmas, I'm sure.'

This was much from Miss Jane, who couldn't help speaking shortly, even when she was pleased. Katy withdrew in high glee.

But that night, just before bed-time, something happened so surprising that Katy, telling Clover of it afterward, said she half fancied that she must have dreamed it all. It was about eight o'clock in the evening: she was passing down Quaker Row, and Miss Jane called and asked her to come in. Miss Jane's cheeks were flushed, and she spoke fast, as if she had resolved to say something, and thought the sooner it was over the better.

'Miss Carr,' she began, 'I wish to tell you that I made up my mind some time since that we did you an injustice last term. It is not your attentions to me during my illness which have changed my opinion, that was done before I fell ill. It is your general conduct, and the good influence which I have seen you exert over other girls, which convinced me that we must have been wrong about you. That is all. I thought you might like to hear me say this, and I shall say the same to Mrs. Nipson.'

'Thank you,' said Katy, 'you don't know how glad I am!' She half thought she would kiss Miss Jane, but somehow it didn't seem possible; so she shook hands very heartily instead, and flew to her room, feeling as if her feet were wings.

'It seems too good to be true. I want to cry, I am so happy,' she told Clover. 'What a lovely day this has been!'

And of all that she had received, I think Katy considered this explanation with Miss Jane as her very best Christmas box.

Susan Coolidge | from What Katy Did at School

7

October

National Poetry Day

Bending above the spicy woods which blaze,
Arch skies so blue they flash, and hold the sun
Immeasurably far; the waters run
Too slow, so freighted are the river-ways
With gold of elms and birches from the maze
Of forests. Chestnuts, clicking one by one,
Escape from satin burs; her fringes done,
The gentian spreads them out in sunny days,
And, like late revelers at dawn, the chance
Of one sweet, mad, last hour, all things assail,
And conquering, flush and spin; while, to enhance
The spell, by sunset door, wrapped in a veil
Of red and purple mists, the summer, pale,
Steals back alone for one more song and dance.

Helen Hunt Jackson | 'October'

9

October

World Post Day

Take a clean sheet of paper.

A pen or a pencil that feels nice in your hand.

Sit in your favourite spot.

Fill your mind for a moment with everyone you know and love.

Write their names on your piece of paper.

Now you have the start of your Christmas list.

. . .

If you are a super-organised person, or want to be sending cards and parcels overseas, today is a good prompt for making plans, or beginning to set them in motion.

First Friday of October

~ World Smile Day ~

Do an act of kindness. Help one person smile.

Designer Harvey Ball created World Smile Day in 1999 – 'his other really great idea' after his 1963 smiley-face campaign for State Mutual which went on to become an international symbol for goodwill and happiness.

'The smiley face knows no politics, no geography and no religion. Harvey's idea was that for at least one day each year, neither should we.'

10

October

Mental Health Day

Hands, do what you're bid:
Bring the balloon of the mind
That bellies and drags in the wind
Into its narrow shed.

W. B. Yeats | 'The Balloon of the Mind'

12

October

Dia de la Raza, Indigenous Peoples Day

Once a national holiday to mark the anniversary of Christopher Columbus' arrival on 12 October 1492, an increasing number of countries in the Americas and several states in the US now use this date to celebrate the cultures of Indigenous peoples and recognise the importance of their sustainable land use in fighting climate change and building resilience to natural disasters.

Through a little hole in the wall the children had crept in, and they were sitting in the branches of the trees. In every tree that [the Giant] could see there was a little child. And the trees were so glad to have the children back again that they had covered themselves with blossoms, and were waving their arms gently above the children's heads. The birds were flying about and twittering with delight, and the flowers were looking up through the green grass and laughing. It was a lovely scene, only in one corner it was still winter. It was the farthest corner of the garden, and in it was standing a little boy. He was so small that he could not reach up to the branches of the tree, and he was wandering all round it, crying bitterly. The poor tree was still quite covered with frost and snow, and the North Wind was blowing and roaring above it. 'Climb up! little boy,' said the Tree, and it bent its branches down as low as it could; but the boy was too tiny.

And the Giant's heart melted as he looked out. 'How selfish I have been!' he said; 'now I know why the Spring would not come here. I will put that poor little boy on the top of the tree, and then I will knock down the wall, and my garden shall be the children's playground for ever and ever.' He was really very sorry for what he had done.

So he crept downstairs and opened the front door quite softly, and went out into the garden. But when the children saw him they were so frightened that they all ran away, and the garden became winter again. Only the little boy did not run, for his eyes were so full of tears that he did not see the Giant coming. And the Giant stole up behind him and took him gently in his hand, and put him up into the tree. And the tree broke at once into blossom, and the birds came and sang on it, and the little boy stretched out his two arms and flung them round the Giant's neck, and kissed him. And the other children, when they saw that the Giant was not wicked any longer, came running back, and with them came the Spring. 'It is your garden now, little children,' said the Giant, and he took a great axe and knocked down the wall. And when the people were going to market at twelve o'clock they found the Giant playing with the children in the most beautiful garden they had ever seen.

All day long they played, and in the evening they came to the Giant to bid him good-bye.

'But where is your little companion?' he said: 'the boy I put into the tree.' The Giant loved him the best because he had kissed him.

'We don't know,' answered the children; 'he has gone away.'

'You must tell him to be sure and come here tomorrow,' said the Giant. But the children said that they did not know where he lived, and had never seen him before; and the Giant felt very sad.

~

Every afternoon, when school was over, the children came and played with the Giant. But the little boy whom the Giant loved was never seen again.

The Giant was very kind to all the children, yet he longed for his first little friend, and often spoke of him. 'How I would like to see him!' he used to say.

~

Years went over, and the Giant grew very old and feeble. He could not play about any more, so he sat in a huge armchair, and watched the children at their games, and admired his garden. 'I have many beautiful flowers,' he said; 'but the children are the most beautiful flowers of all.'

~

One winter morning he looked out of his window as he was dressing. He did not hate the Winter now, for he knew that it was merely the Spring asleep, and that the flowers were resting.

Suddenly he rubbed his eyes in wonder, and looked and looked. It certainly was a marvellous sight. In the farthest corner of the garden was a tree quite covered with lovely white blossoms. Its branches were all golden, and silver fruit hung down from them, and underneath it stood the little boy he had loved.

12 October is Oscar Wilde's birthday.

Oscar Wilde | *from* The Selfish Giant

Third week of October

~ Erfoud Date Harvest Festival ~

A three-day carnival is held each year in Erfoud, Morocco, to celebrate the harvest of around a million date trees.

Opulent, sticky and sweet, dates are said to protect from poison and witchcraft. Richly nutritious, they are served at the Ramadan iftar table, for breaking the fast at sunset each day.

We have been eating dates for over 6,000 years, whether plucked soft or dry straight from the palm tree, stuffed, baked into cookies, jewel-like in puddings, or slow-cooked into a tender tagine.

~

> Mary when she withdrew from her family to a place in the east . . . Then the pains of labour drove her to the trunk of a palm tree. She cried 'Alas! I wish I had died before this, and was a thing long forgotten!'
>
> So a voice reassured her from below her, 'Do not grieve! Your Lord has provided a stream at your feet. And shake a trunk of this palm tree towards you, it will drop fresh, ripe dates upon you. So eat and drink, and put your heart at ease.'
>
> *Qu'ran* 'Maryam' 19:22–19:26

21

October

Apple Day

Heirloom heritage apple tree varieties have such great names. Look out for orchards and farmers markets holding apple-tastings nearby, to see if they taste as good as they sound!

Cornish Gilliflower ~ Nutmeg Pippin ~ Worcester Pearmain

Lemon Pippin ~ Ashmead's Kernel ~ American Mother

William Crump ~ Rivers Early Peach ~ Laxton's Superb

Fall Russet ~ Holstein ~ Red Ellison's Orange

Saint Cecilia ~ Irish Peach ~ Alkmene ~ Yellow Ingestrey

Kerry Pippin ~ St Edmund's Pippin ~ Margaret ~ Sunset

~

Apples for Christmas

Wrapped in coloured paper, *pingguo* apples are a popular gift to give in China on Ping'an Ye, 'peaceful/quiet evening' – Christmas Eve – because their names sound so similar.

Give a decorated apple to someone you like at Midnight Mass – or cut one in half across the middle after your Christmas meal: if the pips at its heart form the shape of a star, it means good health.

Hang them in the trees as bird food for 'animal Christmas'.

21/22/23
October

The sun enters loyal, mysterious, passionate

~ SCORPIO ~

Heal and transform.

. . .

Month of the

~ PIG ~

Diligent, compassionate, responsible, generous.

25
October

All children are artists. The problem is how to
remain an artist once you grow up.

Pablo Picasso (attributed)

~

Take a line for a walk on Picasso's birthday.

Maybe you're not going to be illustrating your own
Christmas cards, but why should kids have all the fun
with glitter?

Set aside thoughts of whether what you're making is
'good' or 'bad' and just enjoy the process – doodle,
squiggle, draw stars and Christmas trees and little houses
that might be made of gingerbread.

Take scissors and an old magazine, hack away at the
Christmas catalogues that come tumbling through the
door around this time of year. Make a mood board or a
collage or just a glorious mess.

28

October

Month of the Reed begins in the Celtic Tree Calendar

Imaginative ~ Fearless ~ Strong-willed

~

Scattered on floors for their pleasing scent, tightly-packed into thatched roofs or ingeniously woven to form whole dwellings, reeds make music, and paper, and even boats.

They are symbol of protection, purification, communication; and in Ancient Egypt, the journey to the afterlife was envisioned as sailing into a Field of Reeds.

Perhaps there is a field of reeds near you, where you can go and listen to the wind singing and watch the birds and insects who love to shelter there . . .

Third Thursday of October

~ **Spirit Day** ~

Take the pledge against bullying and wear purple
to show your support.

It was at night that the carnival was at its merriest. For the frost continued unbroken; the nights were of perfect stillness; the moon and stars blazed with the hard fixity of diamonds, and to the fine music of flute and trumpet the courtiers danced.

Orlando . . . beheld, coming from the pavilion of the Muscovite Embassy, a figure, which, whether boy's or woman's, for the loose tunic and trousers of the Russian fashion served to disguise the sex, filled him with the highest curiosity. The person, whatever the name or sex, was about middle height, very slenderly fashioned, and dressed entirely in oyster-coloured velvet, trimmed with some unfamiliar greenish-coloured fur.

But these details were obscured by the extraordinary seductiveness which issued from the whole person. Images, metaphors of the most extreme and extravagant twined and twisted in his mind. He called her a melon, a pineapple, an olive tree, an emerald, and a fox in the snow all in the space of three seconds; he did not know whether he had heard her, tasted her, seen her, or all three together . . .

A melon, an emerald, a fox in the snow – so he raved, so he stared. When the boy, for alas, a boy it must be – no woman could skate with such speed and vigour – swept almost on tiptoe past him, Orlando was ready to tear his hair with vexation that the person was of his own sex, and thus all embraces were out of the question. But the skater came closer. Legs, hands, carriage, were a boy's, but no boy ever had a mouth like that; no boy had those breasts; no boy had eyes which looked as if they had been fished from the bottom of the sea. Finally, coming to a stop and sweeping a curtsey with the utmost grace to the King, who was shuffling past on the arm of some Lord-in-waiting, the unknown skater came to a standstill. She was a woman. Orlando stared; trembled; turned hot; turned cold; longed to hurl himself through the summer air; to crush acorns beneath his feet; to toss his arms with the beech trees and the oaks.

Virginia Woolf | *from* Orlando

31
October

Hallowe'en

All Hallows' Eve

Samhain

> The veil between worlds is at its thinnest
> and mischievous fairy-folk are all about . . .

Hallowe'en is the perfect excuse to cuddle up and eat your trick-or-treat sweets in front of your first festive film: it's time for *The Nightmare Before Christmas*!

. . .

Apparently, we should hang horseshoes up the chimney to stop witches flying down. It's luckiest to find one lying by the side of the road (the horseshoe, rather than the witch, I assume; it's not advisable to disturb a snoozing witch . . .).

31
October

La Castanyada ~ Chestnut Festival

In the Middle Ages, on All Hallows' Eve, Catalonian bell-ringers rang bells for the dead through the night, and their neighbours would bring nuts, cookies, sweets and wine to the church. But most especially they'd bring *castanas* – chestnuts – which give their name to the celebration that still continues today.

In Italy, the chestnut tree was known as 'the bread tree' and it nourished entire populations in the mountains. It is traditional to eat chestnuts on All Saints' Day, 1 November, leaving some on the table for deceased loved ones. They are a precious gift for baptism, and a gesture of hospitality towards guests at weddings.

American chestnuts were once one of the most abundant trees in North America, cultivated by Native American peoples as a main food crop, although over-use for building as well as chestnut blight have now left them critically endangered.

In Japan, chestnuts are the fruit of the autumn, along with pears and grapes. Served as part of the New Year's menu, they represent mastery and strength, hard times and good.

~

Accompany your chestnuts with a glass of Moscatell, panellets (small sweets of marzipan, almonds and pine nuts) or boniatos (sweet potatoes). Enjoy them roasted (over an open fire if you can!), boiled, cooked in rice, ground as flour, flipped into crepes, candied or puréed, the delicious sweetness of glacéd marrons.

Rich in vitamins and minerals, with a wonderful creamy texture, they make the perfect heart of a vegan feast.

Buy them hot and blackened, wrapped in newspaper, from street stalls.

To toast your own, score the rounded 'belly' side with an X – just deep enough to cut through the first and second skin. Spread them on a baking sheet – or even better, in a chestnut roasting pan – and cook on a low heat for 30–40 minutes, or on hot coals or in the ashy part of an open fire, for 15–20 minutes. Keep a close eye on them and turn them or shake the pan a few times to keep them from burning. They're cooked when the skin darkens and the X curls back to reveal the gold-brown flesh inside.

Serve tucked up in cloth in a breadbasket: they're easier to peel when they're still warm!

In the Southern Hemisphere,
the wheel of the year is turning to summer

~ BELTANE ~

'Bright Fire'

A celebration of fire, sun, new life
and the coming of summer.

Abundance ~ Regrowth ~ Renewal

Dress a tree | watch the sun rise | wear flowers in your hair or in your pockets or buttonhole | leap a bonfire | wash your face in morning dew | make a wish | dress up as the man in green | dance | sing | make merry | make a change, if you want

All of life is bursting with potency.

In the Northern Hemisphere,
the dark half of the year begins

~ SAMHAIN ~

'End of Summer'

Closure ~ Rebirth

Bake soul cakes | bob for apples | feast on cider, game, nuts and berries | make a protective autumn wreath | connect with your ancestors | breathe in the scent of rosemary, for remembrance | burn a white candle at the window, to help guide the spirits back to their world

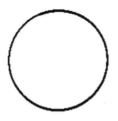

October / November

– Festivals –

that move with the Moon

Here are some of the festivals that usually occur
around mid-October to mid-November – check this year's
calendar to find out exactly when . . .

New Moon

Try to find some quiet this dark moon day.

Draw on the passionate energy of **Scorpio**.
Look within to truly understand the depths of your
    feelings.
Build a greater awareness of those around you.
A time for reflection, meditation, introspection.

Eat simple foods – milk, water, fruit and nuts, soup.

Light a candle at sunset.

Set intentions.
With the new moon: to find ways to express what is in
    your heart.
With the full moon: to eliminate bad habits and
    influences from your life.

Let go of old and tired things, make space for new and
    exciting beginnings.

It can feel as though everyone wants something from us at this time of year: to buy things from them, spend time with them, remember to send cards to them, donate time or money to them . . .

We charge about the place visiting people, staying up way past bedtime, cramming in shopping and cooking and DIY and cleaning and a million other tasks that we've been putting off for months but now feel we must urgently do 'before Christmas'.

We forget that, as well as being 'the most wonderful time of the year', these months can also lay us low with seasonal depression, or bring new waves of grief. FOMO can make us ache with loneliness, and there's usually at least one nasty bug going round.

Take a moment of peace in your home. Treat yourself to the kind of welcome you would give a valued guest.

Make a list – or more – of everything you are looking forward to: the films to watch, music to listen to, board games to play. Think about who it lifts your heart to see.

Perhaps while you're writing you might like to have a cup of tea, or hot chocolate; a slice of cake or a sweet restorative date. Make yourself comfy!

~ Diwali ~

The five-day festival is timed around the new moon, with feasts and fireworks sometimes lasting all night.

Celebrate light over darkness, knowledge over ignorance, the triumph of good over evil.

Day One ~ **Dhanteras**
Cleaning, preparing the home. A lucky day to go to markets and buy gold or new things for the kitchen.

Day Two ~ **Choti Diwali**
Decorating the home, stringing lights and creating rangolis – intricate, brightly coloured floor paintings.

Day Three ~ **Diwali & Lakshmi Puja**
Celebration of the Goddess Lakshmi, for happiness, prosperity and fame. Light clay *diyas* and oil lamps, and offer flowers, fruits (water chestnuts, pomegranate, quince, coconut) and *kesari bhaat* semolina pudding with saffron, nuts and sugar.

Day Four ~ **Padwa**
Celebrations of the love between husband and wife.

Day Five ~ **Bhal Duj**
Celebrations of brothers and sisters.

~ Festivals of Lights ~

From Zhon Qui Jie to Thadingyut, Diwali to Chanukah/Hanukkah and Christmas itself, every culture has its festival of dark nights made light, or bright nights made brighter. Symbols of hope, welcome, delight and togetherness. Commemorations of times when light was a miracle . . .

Traditional devotional lamps are simple pinch pots handmade in clay or even flour and water paste shaped into a palm-sized saucer with a little pinched spout to hold the wick, and left to dry out overnight. They are filled with olive oil lit with a strip of cotton wick, or a *bati* twist of cotton wool soaked in melted ghee.

Hanging- and carrying-lantern shades originally made from bamboo and paper or silk, lit with candles, have evolved with the arts of painting, paper-cutting and needlework, becoming ever more elaborate and beautiful, although the iconic full-moon-shaped red globes remain the eternal symbol of wholeness and prosperity.

Decorate paper lampshades with your own wishes, riddles, pictures and blessings. Put tea lights, floating candles or a jumble of fairy lights in glass jars and bowls, or into old tin cans and pierce patterns into the sides.

There is so much joy to be had with lights; and pretty much anything looks beautiful in the soft golden light of a flame.

Just remember: never leave your burning lamps unattended.

Marigolds ~ Mary's Gold

Genda ~ Herb of the Sun

Flor de Muerto ~ Flower of the dead

Health-giving and insect-repelling, mood-lifting and stress-relieving, golden marigold flowers are synonymous with Diwali and with Dia de los Muertos festivals.

They bloomed year-round in monastery gardens to adorn altars, and were used to colour baked treats as a more affordable alternative to saffron.

If you're lucky enough to live near an abundance of these glorious yellow blooms, thread them into garlands to adorn your doorways; float them in bowls; scatter them on every surface.

If you have the time one year – and perhaps some other willing crafters to help – you can learn how to fold them from crepe paper, creating your own string of sunshine, to keep forever and bring out for every festival.

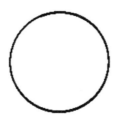

Full Hunter's Moon

Drying Rice Moon

Falling Leaves Moon

Freezing Moon

Ice Moon

Migrating Moon

Travel Moon

Dying Moon

~

Strength & Endurance ~ Protection ~ Guidance ~ Transition

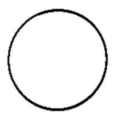

~ Festival of the Full Moon ~

A day of abundance and prosperity

Take a holy bath

Pause to watch the moon rise

Donate food and clothes if you can

Float a light in a little boat

~ Nabanna – 'new rice' harvest festival ~

Greet the moon with lamps

Eat rice cakes

Give children gifts and sweetened milk

Offer rice and food to crows

Celebrate with food, dance and music

Blow loudly through a conch shell

17 & 27

Cheshvan

(second month of the Hebrew calendar)

The month of Cheshvan is the beginning of the rainy season in the Land of Israel.

On the seventeenth day of the second month – on that day all the springs of the great deep burst forth, and the floodgates of the heavens were opened. And rain fell on the earth forty days and forty nights.

On that very day Noah and his sons, Shem, Ham and Japheth, together with his wife and the wives of his three sons, entered the ark. They had with them every wild animal according to its kind, all livestock according to their kinds, every creature that moves along the ground according to its kind and every bird according to its kind, everything with wings. Pairs of all creatures that have the breath of life in them came to Noah and entered the ark.

. . .

The waters flooded the earth for a hundred and fifty days. But God remembered Noah and all the wild animals and the livestock that were with him in the ark, and he sent a wind over the earth, and the waters receded.

...

After forty days Noah opened a window he had made in the ark and sent out a raven, and it kept flying back and forth until the water had dried up from the earth. Then he sent out a dove to see if the water had receded from the surface of the ground . . . When the dove returned to him in the evening, there in its beak was a freshly plucked olive leaf. Then Noah knew that the water had receded from the earth.

...

By the twenty-seventh day of the second month the earth was completely dry.

...

So Noah came out, together with his sons and his wife and his sons' wives. All the animals and all the creatures that move along the ground and all the birds – everything that moves on land – came out of the ark, one kind after another.

...

The Lord said in his heart . . . 'As long as the earth endures, seedtime and harvest, cold and heat, summer and winter, day and night will never cease.'

Genesis 7: 11-8, 22

~ Lhabab Duchen, Duchen Festival ~

Buddha's 'descent to earth from heaven' after visiting his mother.

A day for acts of kindness and generosity.

The Noble Eightfold Path:

1. Right action (behaving skilfully);
2. Right speech (speaking truthfully);
3. Right livelihood (causing no harm or suffering to others);
4. Right mindfulness (being aware of yourself, and of others' feelings);
5. Right effort (putting effort into positive emotions);
6. Right concentration (developing focus for meditation);
7. Right understanding (remembering that actions have consequences);
8. Right intention.

~ Gurpurab Guru Nanak Jayanti ~
celebration of the founder of Sikhism

The three pillars upon which Guru Nanak built Sikhism are Naam Japna (devotion), Kirat Karni (living an honest life) and Chakna (being generous to those in need and to communities).

Wonderful are the beings, wonderful are the species.
Wonderful are the forms, wonderful are the colours.
Wonderful are the beings who wander around naked.
Wonderful is the wind, wonderful is the water.
Wonderful is fire, which works wonders.
Wonderful is the earth, wonderful the sources of creation.
Wonderful are the tastes to which mortals are attached.
Wonderful is union, and wonderful is separation.
Wonderful is hunger, wonderful is satisfaction.
Wonderful is His Praise, wonderful is His adoration.
Wonderful is the wilderness, wonderful is the path.
Wonderful is closeness, wonderful is distance.
How wonderful to behold the Lord, ever-present here.
Beholding His wonders, I am wonder-struck.

Guru Nanak | *from* 'Asa di Vaar' (Ballad of Hope)

It's witches' new year.
All over the world, cultures honour their dead and
begin a month of remembrance.
In the thrill of the dark, we throw festivals of lights;
bonfires call us close – but not too close!

The earth tucks itself up under layers of frost that cloak the North, living on quietly, building strength beneath the ground.
As the sun burns on the Southern Hemisphere, there is respite in cool shade.
Rest ~ find peace.

The south wall warms me: November has begun,
Yet never shone the sun as fair as now
While the sweet last-left damsons from the bough
With spangles of the morning's storm drop down
Because the starling shakes it, whistling what
Once swallows sang.

Edward Thomas | *from* 'There's Nothing Like the Sun'

THE AIR seems to sizzle with party time in November. Hallowe'en kicks it off, and Diwali showers firework sparkles all around. Life is late-night, twinkling lights, sweet treats, with well-deserved good times to come.

It's birthday season in our family, so it's present-hunting month. I make pilgrimages to my favourite places – the department stores with the best window displays, the gorgeous independent shops where everything is picked with care, my lovely locals where they know their customers by name and host late-night openings with mulled wine and mince pies as you browse. I love it when you spot the perfect thing, then sneak into the house with bags full of secrets, finding hiding places for treasures so as not to spoil the surprise.

Mother Christmas starts her Christmas baking: steeping dried fruit for mincemeat ready to pop into pies, stirring up plum pudding and feeding the Christmas cake, carefully peeling back its layers of tinfoil and parchment to slosh on the brandy that keeps it so good. She makes two, so she only has to bake pudding and cake every other year: if you look after them well, they are even better for the keeping.

The Elves are at the Christmas markets, running stalls or stocking up on stocking fillers. They have an eye on last posting dates, for anything that needs to reach overseas, and unlike me they keep careful lists of what they have bought, maybe even checking against their records from last year and the year before, to be sure not to give the same thing twice.

In my mother's desk I found notebooks and lists of dinner party menus and guests, gifts given and received, going back years – a record of all that thoughtful love and generous creativity she poured into her family and friends, as wonderful as any diary. November was her birthday, and she loved a party more than anything.

~ Presents ~

Gifts are in the thought. Sometimes in the time taken. In the meaning given. The perfect present says 'this person gets me' . . . or is that little treat you'd never buy yourself.

~

There are many different traditions around gift-giving, but you can be pretty sure that for most people, in every culture, in every part of the world, exchanging presents will play a part in special days.

And in Mali, the tradition of *dama* makes gift-giving part of everyday life. Though generally poor in cash, Malians reserve the greatest reverence for generosity and a strong, informal women's social network lies at the heart of what's called a 'gift economy', a web of relationships and community that stretches way beyond material objects.

This sounds wonderful to me, caught up as I am in what can feel like spiralling commercialised pressure to spend more money than I can afford on ever more elaborate and extravagant gifts. However much I promise myself that this year I will reign myself in, I get an undeniable, addictive dopamine rush watching someone I love light up with joy at unwrapping my parcel. Just as I can find myself consumed with Fear of Missing Out when I hear about all the parties and pantos I'm not at, I tangle myself in Dread of Disappointing when it comes to giving presents. Although it's one of my greatest pleasures, the pressure to find the perfect present can send my joyful anticipation for Christmas tipping into anxiety faster than it takes to find the end of the sellotape.

It's not like this for everyone. I particularly like the sound of spending Christmas in the Dominican Republic, where I hear that no material gifts are given on Christmas Day – the only things you are allowed to give are food, wine and quality time.

What to give?

In Mali, a gift might be a meal for a hungry neighbour, change for a bus fare, a bracelet.

Food – especially sweets, sweet treats, chocolate and fruit – makes a popular gift all over the world. New clothes are given and worn on special occasions everywhere, and new tools and utensils are a useful expression of generosity (assuming it's something that will actually be used!). And, of course, money – whether pinned to bridal clothing, thrown like confetti, or tucked into special envelopes – is always welcome (although I confess I struggle to know how much – is there a code for these things? To me, the joy of giving an object is that the recipient might not be aware of the cost; I love to buy presents in the sales, because it means I can give something worth more than I could otherwise spend.)

Before you hit the stores in a panicked frenzy and end up buying any old tat just so you have something – anything – to wrap, it might be good to take a moment and think:

What are the best presents you've ever received?

What would be a real little treat for them, something they wouldn't buy for themselves?

Think about their life stage and whether they need more things or are trying to declutter.

Are they still experimenting with skincare and would love to try products they can't normally afford, or have they found what works for them and don't really like to change? What do you think they'd like to use but can't justify buying for themselves?

What have you noticed about the things they like, what they have at home or in their bathroom? Do they tend to go for spicy or citrusy or floral?

Does everybody always give them scarves or socks or the same thing every time and would they be thrilled to get something different this year?

Decide whether the clichés are actually a good thing sometimes: what can you never have too much of?

Present ideas

- ☆ Things that elevate your everyday
- ☆ Beautiful pair of scissors
- ☆ Beautiful box of matches
- ☆ My mother-in-law once gave me a handy DIY kit of hammer, tape measure and scissors all with lovely William Morris decorative handles. Distinctively mine, and distinctly handy, they remind me of her whenever I use them, and they make little chores a pleasure.
- ☆ A box of art supplies, or just one extra special pencil. A heavy brass sharpener or an old-school eraser that rubs out really well.
- ☆ A tin opener that actually works. Those ingenious herb scissors with multiple blades. Comedy rubber gloves, novelty washing-up brush, superstar-baker apron.
- ☆ Nutmeg grater, olive spoon, pickle fork
- ☆ A bowl that will make them happy over breakfast in the morning
- ☆ Tray (a little individual one, something bright for sharing, a lap tray with a beanbag base or fold-out legs)
- ☆ One of the best presents ever was a set of champagne

boule glasses that my friend had collected over weeks and months from charity shops. There was so much thought there; she knew that I loved the shape of them and would relish the eclectic mix of patterns and styles.

- ☆ Warm hat, gloves, slippers, blankets, cosy comforting things
- ☆ Even socks, if they're soft and gorgeous and a cut above what you might buy yourself
- ☆ A knife roll, a jewellery roll, a really beautiful lavender bag. Oven gloves that feel special, tea towels that you might put on your wall as a piece of art (or that make you laugh at some private shared joke).
- ☆ Candles – in striking colours, or golden-glowing beeswax
- ☆ Fairy lights, a portable Bluetooth speaker
- ☆ Photographs, whether framed or not
- ☆ Mementos from a place or an experience you had together – buy them secretly from the gift shop while you're there and hide them away for later . . .
- ☆ Anything for kids that feels 'grown up': a wooden or metal toolbox with a carry-handle and lots of little compartments they can fill with all their treasures, a proper 'artists roll' for their pens and pencils, some makeup to experiment with, or posh moisturiser, a wallet, a smart-key fob
- ☆ If you don't know them well, it's wise to steer clear of things that are trend-based unless you know it's what they want: it's so easy to get it wrong, and even if the last time you saw them it was all they were obsessed with, there's a very good chance they've moved on . . .
- ☆ A game that all the family can play, a puzzle to do together
- ☆ Vouchers and money

- ☆ Chocolate and sweets, posh biscuits and crackers for cheese
- ☆ Homemade chutney, jam, sloe gin (whether you made it yourself or found it at a local shop or Christmas fair)
- ☆ Booze is good, when appropriate – if they don't drink it themselves, they can serve it to others or take it on to the next party they go to
- ☆ A poinsettia, hyacinths, potted herbs or flowers
- ☆ Jewellery doesn't need to be expensive to be meaningful
- ☆ In fact, in general, presents don't need to be expensive to be meaningful: experiences, the promise of time together, 'vouchers' to redeem for babysitting or DIY help or a walk in the park

When do you do your shopping?

Mother Christmas had a special present drawer, always stocked with little things to be quickly wrapped when a gift was called for.

My dad and husband do their Christmas shopping on Christmas Eve, and I think there's actually something to be said for compressing the stress into just that one day.

The Elves will have everything bought and wrapped (and labelled so they don't have to unwrap it again to remember what's inside) by September – essential if October to December is a busy working time that doesn't leave much room for anything else.

When do you give?

Socks or shoes left out each Advent night for sweetie presents that magically appear the next morning . . . After a visit from St Nicholas on 5 or 6 December . . . At the sound of a bell ringing or at sight of the first star or after Mass on Christmas Eve . . . Stockings first thing on Christmas morning, one present before church, wait to open the rest once the turkey is safely in the oven and Mother Christmas can get away from the kitchen . . . New Year's Eve, New Year's Day, Three Kings Day . . . this really is The Time of Gifts. And if you have me as a godmother, you will get your presents at some random point when I finally get round to posting them or paying a visit! Perhaps it is comforting to know there are so many different traditions and you can tap into the one that works for you. And to remember that no gift is unwelcome, however late it comes, as long as it is given with care and thoughtfulness.

~ Present-wrapping ~

Mother Christmas once worked in Harrods as a gift-wrapper, and our gifts were like works of art – little pyramid packages, ribbons in perfect bows, cloud-like layers of tissue-paper lining, edges always crisply folded and tucked, never left raw . . . Apparently the secret is in cutting the paper to the correct size and using the smallest possible piece of tape.

Sadly, I don't seem to have inherited the wrapping gift. The harder I try, the scrappier the parcel seems to turn out. Also they have a tendency to ping open before they should, on account of trying not to spoil the aesthetic with great slabs of sticky tape . . .

So, I'm wondering: could we all just make a pact to use gift-bags and not write on the labels and keep on using them again and again until the silk cord handles have frayed and they're all battered and well loved?

Or master the art of Japanese *furoshiki* and fold our gifts in beautiful pieces of cloth.

Every year I vow that I'll get the sewing machine out and use up all the bits of fabric I inherited from my mother and stitch them into lovely bags with ribbon ties.

One day, maybe, perhaps.

Wrapping supplies

I'm a hoarder of little bits and bobs that might be useful one day. It's a tendency I inherited from my parents – along with my mother's own store of make-do-and-mend supplies.

As a sort of therapy, one particularly fraught day I tackled the drawer filled with tangled ribbons and string and sorted them by colour into old jam jars. They're still in tangles, despite my best intentions to roll them neatly (I still have a few that my ma – or perhaps it was even my granny – secured neatly with those little white wire things you use to tie up freezer bags. I can't bear to unroll them to use, of course. I love the little stab of love I get when they come tumbling out in the chaos of slippery satin and grosgrain). There's something deeply gorgeous about ribbons, and my drawer full of ribbon jars is a secret source of happiness.

Stock up on sellotape – both types, shiny and matte (you can get excellent biodegradable tapes these days, by the way) and brown paper parcel tape.

Brown paper packaging is also handy to have, whether or not you tie it with string.

Look out for rolls of wrapping paper in the sales and keep them for next year.

While I'm a great advocate of reusing, no one else in the house is prepared to hunt through the scraps for just the right size piece, and, anyway, sometimes you have that Big Present that all kids of any age (0–101) are most delighted by, and that does call for a crisp new roll of shiny paper. There's something so satisfying about making a little cut and then gliding your scissors through the paper and trying to stop it from curling immediately back into its scroll for long enough to get the present inside.

Do you have a wrapping ritual?

My friend spends an evening with her daughter every year. They put on their cosy Christmas slipper socks (I imagine they do this whatever the temperature), play carols as loud as the speakers will go and the neighbours will allow, lay on copious bowls of snacks, and get wrapping.

This requires a level of organisation I don't have. I like to shut myself away on Christmas Eve, inevitably a whole lot later than planned, maybe with a little tot of Santa's sherry and a mince pie, and try to find creative solutions when I realise someone else has got there sooner and there's only the cardboard reel left on the sellotape dispenser . . . Hoarder's drawer of ribbons to the rescue!

The unwrapping

Do you love to rip open the paper with glee, flinging it about the room in a frenzy of abandoned delight? Or do you relish the moment, enjoying the packet almost more than the surprise it holds, slicing through the sellotape with a surgeon's precision, carefully smoothing and folding the paper, rolling the ribbon and setting it to one side to be used again, almost as good as new?

I still remember my dad reading out a story from the paper, of a man who'd wrapped all his wife's presents in newspaper one year, including the pristine sheets of wrapping paper within. How we laughed! (But also thought – what an ingenious idea!)

~ Christmas Card Etiquette ~

Who do you send cards to? The rule when we were growing up seemed to be: not to people you see in person, although that always made for little moments of awkwardness when others handed them over to us.

We used to have a Christmas postbox in school, handmade in battered cardboard and covered with red paper, patched up good-as-new each year. Everyone would send cards to everyone and the excitement of the daily delivery was only matched by the thrill of being in the top year and getting to be the ones who were allowed to open up the postbox and sort the avalanche of post that came sliding out.

For a while into adulthood I continued the approach of sending cards to pretty much all in my address book. Only, these days when people move they tend to let you know by email, or was it a text or something on Messenger? Come November you can't remember if it was them who moved at all or somebody else and is that illegible scribble in the book their new address or the old one? When did you last update the entry on your phone? Should you just send the card anyway and hope someone will forward it on? What's their new surname? And what's the name of their partner/children/dog and can you get away without mentioning them or is that rude?

Breathe.

If you are that much out of touch, why are they on your list of people to send cards to? Is it because you regret letting things drift? If you still have their number, or email address, could you ping them a message and pick things up again? Because maybe a Christmas card sent out into the blue isn't the best way to do that. Or perhaps you have both moved on, and it's okay to have happy memories without the obligation of updating the mailing list.

Of course, there's the inevitable pang when you get the card from them – with no return address, of course . . . At which point, you can ask yourself again: is the pang because I'd really like to be still in touch? Or a little twinge of guilt that I can acknowledge and then move on?

So: if you do send cards (and it's okay if you don't), be sure to put a return address on the envelope; that way, they have yours, and if it gets 'returned to sender' then at least you'll know they've moved on.

Catching the post

Mother Christmas would dedicate a day, or even two, to sitting at her desk with fountain pen and blotter, writing her Christmas cards.

I've tried various techniques, from taking the pressure off by sending New Year cards instead, to catching the post on 1 December, to writing and sending as I receive them to the people who have sent them to me. There was even a year I finally posted the cards I had written, addressed, sealed and stamped the year before but never got round to taking to the postbox. For whatever reason, I find Christmas-card-sending a real struggle. Perhaps it's a generational thing. I do love the newsy email I get from the neighbours who moved away years ago, the animated digital cards, the unexpected note from someone you wish you hadn't lost touch with. I just can't seem to get my act together to send them myself.

I long to spread that joy, and I comfort myself that a card is lovely to receive, at any time of year; maybe even more so when it's out of the blue . . .

~ Party Season ~

Drinks parties, office parties, dinner parties, charity gala events . . . We love a party at this time of year. The media get us in a froth about whether our bodies and wardrobes are party-ready; and they help us out with life-saving advice on office-to-party transformations. Some of my favourite nights out were because of that strange camaraderie that comes from getting changed in the ladies', sharing hairbrushes and mascara and compliments, marvelling at the transformation from buttoned-up business-wear to one-night-only glam.

Our mantra in those days was 'keep yourself nice' and sometimes we even managed it. There was a lot of free and free-flowing alcohol and not very much by way of food, and it's probably just as well that I don't remember much of it apart from the fantastic liberation that comes from dancing like nobody's watching to cheesy music with people you know and, at least in that moment, love and then staggering on to karaoke or this little place somebody knows that's open all night and trying to hail the last black cab home or running for the night bus and making it and watching the lights of the city flash past and feeling like you're living in a movie and knowing you'll get to relive it all again with all the juicy bits round the water cooler tomorrow.

Party planning

If you're hosting, keep it simple. Arrange things so you don't spend the whole time in the kitchen or checking coats and booking cabs – unless you want to. Cater with showstopping canapés if you love to cook; but everyone will forgive you if you don't have the time or inclination. Parties are about the people and the atmosphere – and that begins with a relaxed and smiling host.

Accepting help

We're so conditioned to say, 'No, it's fine, you sit down and have a good time, it's Christmas, you're here to enjoy yourself' that we overlook two things: first, it's really hard to enjoy yourself if your host is having some kind of passsive-aggressive meltdown in the kitchen; second, people tend not to offer help if they don't want to give it. And have you ever thought that perhaps you're doing them a favour? Perhaps what they're really asking is: can I come and hide in here with you instead of making awkward polite conversation with your relatives because you're the person I travelled all this way to be with?

Unless, of course, you're the one avoiding the awkward polite conversation, in which case hide away. Especially if the person offering to disturb your personal space is liable to hold forth about how their mother used to do things, or offer helpful advice about the size of the pan you're using, the temperature you've got the oven at, the likelihood of it all being ready together at the same time . . .

I have some surprisingly lovely memories of working together with friends and family, prepping veg while belting out carols; or chatting about the meaning of life while helping with the washing-up. Maybe remembering that, you'll be more likely to say yes the next time someone offers to help. Maybe you'll even ask for help when you need it, and you'll all be glad that you did.

Think about things so that when someone asks if they can help and whether they can bring anything, your mind doesn't go blank and you're ready to answer, Yes, please, it would be brilliant if you could . . .

- ☆ Bring pudding/crisps/dips/vegan course/drinks/sleeping bags/some extra chairs
- ☆ Be in charge of drinks/answering the door
- ☆ Sort out the playlist/party games/seating plan
- ☆ Peel the potatoes
- ☆ Chop the carrots
- ☆ Cut those fiddly little crosses in the bottom of the sprouts that no one knows why but it has to be done
- ☆ Lay the table
- ☆ Fold the napkins using that posh new origami technique only you know how to do
- ☆ Carve the turkey/nut-roast/debone the fish
- ☆ Hand round the veg
- ☆ Clear the table
- ☆ Wash up
- ☆ Dry up
- ☆ Make everyone a nice cup of tea
- ☆ Shove all the wrapping paper in a bag
- ☆ Get some more logs for the fire
- ☆ Pass round the snacks because somehow everyone is hungry, even though half an hour ago we said we couldn't imagine ever wanting to eat again for the rest of our lives we were so stuffed

Party armour

Maybe you're the kind of person who feels at your most alive in a party situation, in which case this will all sound a bit strange. But there are plenty of us who feel awkward in social situations, and it can help to have some strategies to cope.

- ☆ Hand round the canapés: it's a great way to join conversations – and leave them if you want to keep moving

☆ Keep your glass just a quarter full, so you can always escape in search of another drink (be nice and offer them one too) – or use that old fail-safe excuse of needing the loo
☆ Have your answers ready in case:
 — You end up chatting to the boss . . .
 — You get the chance to give your elevator pitch to the person who could give you your big break . . .
 — You want to shut up the judgy people who will never understand you and think it's okay to ask really personal questions . . .
 — You get asked those questions to which your mind always goes blank:
 'What do you want for Christmas?'
 'So, what have you been up to since we last saw you?'
 'What are your plans for the new year?'

Is there anyone you're not looking forward to seeing? Is there anyone you can ask to have your back if you get caught somewhere you don't want to be?

Sometimes, if you're not much looking forward to going but can't politely say no, it's enough to just show your face. A wise man who is excellent at both hosting events and working a room once advised me: find out the guest list in advance if you can, know the three people who need to know you were there, make sure you say hello to them, and then you're free to slip away.

Unless, of course, it's a ten-course sit-down meal with a seating plan and speeches. Then slipping away is harder. I recommend questions: most people are extremely happy to talk about themselves and you might be surprised at what you can learn if you challenge yourself to ask something unexpected.

Down they went, feeling a trifle timid, for they seldom went to parties, and informal as this little gathering was, it was an event to them . . . Meg was at her ease very soon, but Jo, who didn't care much for girls or girlish gossip, stood about, with her back carefully against the wall, and felt as much out of place as a colt in a flower garden. Half a dozen jovial lads were talking about skates in another part of the room, and she longed to go and join them, for skating was one of the joys of her life . . . No one came to talk to her, and one by one the group dwindled away till she was left alone . . . She stared at people rather forlornly till the dancing began. Meg was asked at once, and the tight slippers tripped about so briskly that none would have guessed the pain their wearer suffered smilingly. Jo saw a big red headed youth approaching her corner, and fearing he meant to engage her, she slipped into a curtained recess, intending to peep and enjoy herself in peace.

. . .

'Don't you like to dance, Miss Jo?' Asked Laurie . . .

'I like it well enough if there is plenty of room, and everyone is lively. In a place like this I'm sure to upset something, tread on people's toes, or do something dreadful, so I keep out of mischief and let Meg sail about.'

. . .

'Never mind that. I'll tell you how we can manage. There's a long hall out there, and we can dance grandly, and no one will see us. Please come.'

Jo thanked him and gladly went, wishing she had two neat gloves when she saw the nice, pearl-coloured ones her partner wore. The hall was empty, and they had a grand polka, for Laurie danced well, and taught her the German step, which delighted Jo, being full of swing and spring.

. . .

With many thanks, they said good night and crept in, hoping to disturb no one, but the instant their door creaked, two little nightcaps bobbed up, and two sleepy but eager voices cried out . . .

'Tell about the party! Tell about the party!'

With what Meg called 'a great want of manners' Jo had saved some bonbons for the little girls, and they soon subsided, after hearing the most thrilling events of the evening.

'I declare, it really seems like being a fine young lady, to come home from the party in a carriage and sit in my dressing gown with a maid to wait on me,' said Meg, as Jo bound up her foot with arnica and brushed her hair.

'I don't believe fine young ladies enjoy themselves a bit more than we do, in spite of our burned hair, old gowns, one glove apiece and tight slippers that sprain our ankles when we are silly enough to wear them.' And I think Jo was quite right.

Louisa May Alcott | *from* Little Women

November's

— Special Days —

1
November

Dia de Los Muertos

Celebrated on All Saints' Day and All Souls' Day, the Day of the Dead is rooted in Aztec ritual and the belief that the dead are insulted by sadness and mourning: awakened from their eternal sleep, they dance, feast and party with their loved ones.

5
November

Bonfire Night

let us plot
to use gunpowder
only to celebrate
*

sending sparks showering
in an explosion of peace
*

we will hold hands and walk home
together,
hearts filled
with the reckless beauty we have seen

a.b. | 'Fireworks'

Two days afterwards they carried Matthew Cuthbert over his homestead threshold and away from the fields he had tilled and the orchards he had loved and the trees he had planted; and then Avonlea settled back to its usual placidity and even at Green Gables affairs slipped into their old groove . . . Anne, new to grief, thought it almost sad that it could be so – that they *could* go on in the old way without Matthew. She felt something like shame and remorse when she discovered that the sunrises behind the firs and the pale pink buds opening in the garden gave her the old inrush of gladness when she saw them.

. . .

'It seems like disloyalty to Matthew, somehow, to find pleasure in these things now that he has gone,' she said wistfully to Mrs Allan one evening when they were together in the manse garden. 'I miss him so much – all the time – and yet, Mrs Allan, the world and life seem very beautiful and interesting to me for all. Today Diana said something funny and I found myself laughing. I thought when it happened I could never laugh again. And it somehow seems as if I oughtn't to.'

'When Matthew was here he liked to hear you laugh and he liked to know that you found pleasure in the pleasant things around you,' said Mrs Allan gently. 'He is just away now; and he likes to know it just the same.'

L. M. Montgomery | *from* Anne of Green Gables

11
November

Remembrance Day

They shall grow not old, as we that are left grow old:
Age shall not weary them, nor the years condemn.
At the going down of the sun and in the morning
We will remember them.
. . .
As the stars that shall be bright when we are dust,
Moving in marches upon the heavenly plain;
As the stars that are starry in the time of our darkness,
To the end, to the end, they remain.

Laurence Binyon | *from* 'For the Fallen'

Summer fading, winter comes –
Frosty mornings, tingling thumbs,
Window robins, winter rooks,
And the picture story-books.

Water now is turned to stone
Nurse and I can walk upon;
Still we find the flowing brooks
In the picture story-books.

All the pretty things put by,
Wait upon the children's eye,
Sheep and shepherds, trees and crooks
In the picture story-books.

We may see how all things are,
Seas and cities, near and far,
And the flying fairies' looks,
In the picture story-books.

How am I to sing your praise,
Happy chimney-corner days,
Sitting safe in nursery nooks,
Reading picture story-books?

Robert Louis Stevenson | 'Picture-Books in Winter'

20
November

UNICEF – World Children's Day

How could you help children in need in your local area to have a magical time this year?

Are you able to make a donation of food, presents, pennies or time?

Even giving a little smile can make a big difference!

'**I don't know** what day of the month it is!' said Scrooge. 'I don't know how long I've been among the Spirits. I don't know anything. I'm quite a baby. Never mind. I don't care. I'd rather be a baby. Hallo! Whoop! Hallo here!'

He was checked in his transports by the churches ringing out the lustiest peals he had ever heard. Clash, clang, hammer; ding, dong, bell. Bell, dong, ding; hammer, clang, clash! Oh, glorious, glorious!

Running to the window, he opened it, and put out his head. No fog, no mist; clear, bright, jovial, stirring, cold; cold, piping for the blood to dance to; Golden sunlight; Heavenly sky; sweet fresh air; merry bells. Oh, glorious. Glorious!

'What's today?' cried Scrooge, calling downward to a boy in Sunday clothes, who perhaps had loitered in to look about him.

'EH?' returned the boy, with all his might of wonder.

'What's today, my fine fellow?' said Scrooge.

'Today!' replied the boy. 'Why, CHRISTMAS DAY.'

'It's Christmas Day!' said Scrooge to himself. 'I haven't missed it. The Spirits have done it all in one night. They can do anything they like. Of course they can. Hallo, my fine fellow!'

'Hallo!' returned the boy.

'Do you know the Poulterer's, in the next street but one, at the corner?' Scrooge inquired . . . 'Do you know whether they've sold the prize Turkey that was hanging up there? Not the little prize Turkey: the big one?'

'What, the one as big as me? . . . It's hanging there now,' replied the boy.

'Is it?' said Scrooge. 'Go and buy it . . . tell 'em to bring it here, that I may give them the direction where to take it. Come back with the man, and I'll give you a shilling. Come back with him in less than five minutes and I'll give you half-a-crown!'

The boy was off like a shot . . .

'I'll send it to Bob Cratchit's!' whispered Scrooge, rubbing his hands, and splitting with a laugh. 'He shan't know who sends it. It's twice the size of Tiny Tim . . .'

The hand in which he wrote the address was not a steady one, but write it he did, somehow, and went downstairs to open the street door, ready for the coming of the poulterer's man.

. . .

'Here's the Turkey! Hallo! Whoop! How are you! Merry Christmas!'

It *was* a Turkey! He never could have stood upon his legs, that bird. He would have snapped 'em short off in a minute, like sticks of sealing-wax.

'Why, it's impossible to carry that to Camden Town,' said Scrooge. 'You must have a cab.'

The chuckle with which he said this, and the chuckle with which he paid for the Turkey, and the chuckle with which he paid for the cab, and the chuckle with which he recompensed the boy, were only to be exceeded by the chuckle with which he sat down breathless in his chair again, and chuckled till he cried.

Charles Dickens | *from* A Christmas Carol

Second Saturday of November

~ Arrival of Sinterklaas ~

In a tall bishop's hat and flowing red robes, riding his white horse Ozosnel (Oh-so-Fast), Sinterklaas arrives by boat in the Netherlands from Madrid: the first sighting each year of the children's favourite saint.

Eat *pepernoten* anise and honey cookies and put your shoes out before bedtime each night: you might wake to find they hold chocolate coins or a biscuit in your name letter.

Write a wish list, make a drawing for Sint and his friend Chimney Piet, leave a carrot for Ozosnel; and wait patiently for two weeks to St Nicholas' Eve . . .

22/23

November

The sun enters optimistic, adventurous

~ SAGITTARIUS ~

Try something new.

. . .

Month of the

~ RAT ~

Bright, quick-witted, optimistic, adaptable.

Third Thursday of November

~ **Thanksgiving (US)** ~

Gather your dearest friends and family.

Feast, and raise a toast to all you have to be thankful for.

You ruffled black blossom,
You glossy dark wind.

. . .

Your wattles are the colour of steel-slag which has
    been red-hot
And is going cold,
Cooling to a powdery, pale-oxydised sky-blue.

Why do you have wattles, and a naked, wattled head?
Why do you arch your naked-set eye with a more-
    than-comprehensible arrogance?

The vulture is bald, so is the condor, obscenely,
But only you have thrown this amazing mantilla of
    oxydised sky-blue
And hot red over you:
This queer dross shawl of blue and vermilion,
Whereas the peacock has a diadem.

I wonder why.

. . .

Turkey-cock, turkey-cock
Are you the bird of the next dawn?

D. H. Lawrence | *from* 'Turkey-Cock'

So Christmas came, and with it pleasant memories of home and of home comforts. With it came also news of home – some not of the most pleasant description – and kind wishes from absent friends. 'A merry Christmas to you,' writes one, 'and many of them. Although you will not write to us, we see your name frequently in the newspapers, from which we judge that you are strong and hearty. All your old Jamaica friends are delighted to hear of you, and say that you are an honour to the Isle of Springs.'

I wonder if the people of other countries are as fond of carrying with them everywhere their home habits as the English. I think not. I think there was something purely and essentially English in the determination of the camp to spend the Christmas-day of 1855 after the good old 'home' fashion. It showed itself weeks before the eventful day. In the dinner parties which were got up – in the orders sent to England – in the supplies which came out, and in the many applications made to the hostess of the British Hotel for plum-puddings and mince-pies. The demand for them, and the material necessary to manufacture them, was marvellous. I can fancy that if returns could be got at of the flour, plums, currants, and eggs consumed on Christmas-day in the out-of-the-way Crimean Peninsula, they would astonish us. One determination appeared to have taken possession of every mind – to spend the festive day with the mirth and jollity which the changed prospect of affairs warranted; and the recollection of a year ago, when death and misery were the camp's chief guests, only served to heighten this resolve.

For three weeks previous to Christmas-day, my time was fully occupied in making preparations for it. Pages of my books are filled with orders for plum-puddings and mince-pies, besides which I sold an immense quantity of raw material to those who were too far off to send down for the manufactured article on Christmas-day, and to such purchasers I gave a plain recipe for their guidance. Will the reader take any interest in my Crimean Christmas-pudding? It was plain, but decidedly good. However, you shall judge for yourself: – 'One pound of flour, three-quarters of a pound of raisins, three-quarters of a pound of fat pork, chopped fine, two tablespoonfuls of sugar, a little cinnamon or chopped lemon, half-pint of milk or water; mix these well together, and boil four hours.'

From an early hour in the morning until long after the night had set in, were I and my cooks busy endeavouring to supply the great demand for Christmas fare . . .

I did not get my dinner until eight o'clock, and then I dined in peace off a fine wild turkey or bustard, shot for me on the marshes by the Tchernaya. It weighed twenty-two pounds, and, although somewhat coarse in colour, had a capital flavour.

23 November is Mary Seacole's birthday.

Mary Seacole | *from*
The Wonderful Adventures of Mrs Seacole in Many Lands

The last Sunday before Advent

~ 'Stir-up Sunday' ~

Traditionally the day for making Christmas cakes and puddings, taking its name from the collect – short prayer – read on the twenty-fifth Sunday after Trinity:

> Stir up, we beseech thee, O Lord, the wills of thy faithful people; that they plenteously bringing forth the fruit of good works, may of thee be plenteously rewarded.
>
> The Church of England | Book of Common Prayer

. . . let everyone have a good old stir!

What crowding thoughts around me wake,
What marvels in a Christmas-cake!
Ah say, what strange enchantment dwells
Enclosed within its odorous cells?
Is there no small magician bound
Encrusted in its snowy round?
For magic surely lurks in this,
A cake that tells of vanished bliss;
A cake that conjures up to view
The early scenes, when life was new;
When memory knew no sorrows past,
And hope believed in joys that last! –
Mysterious cake, whose folds contain
Life's calendar of bliss and pain;
That speaks of friends for ever fled,
And wakes the tears I love to shed.
Oft shall I breathe her cherished name
From whose fair hand the offering came:
For she recalls the artless smile
Of nymphs that deck my native isle;
Of beauty that we love to trace,
Allied with tender, modest grace;
Of those who, while abroad they roam,
Retain each charm that gladdens home,
And whose dear friendships can impart
A Christmas banquet for the heart!

Helen Maria Williams | 'To Mrs K, On Her Sending Me an English Christmas Plum-Cake at Paris'

24

November

Month of the Elder begins in the Celtic Tree Calendar

~ The Queen of all Herbs ~

Curious ~ Lively ~ Self-sufficient

Feared by the devil, favoured by foragers, it's said that an elder planted by your house will keep the devil away.

Wild elder is often found near rabbit warrens or badger setts: they help distribute the seeds in their droppings . . .

The word 'elder' is from the Anglo-Saxon word *aeld*, meaning fire. Its hollow stems were used as bellows to blow air into a fire's heart and every part of the tree makes rich dyes: blue and purple from the berries, yellow and green from the leaves, grey and black from the bark.

Harvest the flowers in springtime, and you can drink a toast today with elderflower cordial or champagne.

Be sure to ask the Elder-Mother's permission before you help yourself to any part of her tree!

25

November

Catterntide, feast day of St Catherine of Alexandria

Sveta Kata, Taffy Day, Tire Sainte Catherine

St Catherine is the patron saint of weavers, textile makers, potters and spinners; unmarried girls; intellectuals.

Remembered in a firework, a crochet stitch, a circular window, the shield of an Oxford College, her wheel – with its curved knife blades or hissing spurts of flame on the outer rim – is a symbol of martyrdom, ascension, creation, destruction.

Her holiday marks the beginning of Advent season, and brings luck and safety to cattle and livestock through the winter.

Join the Catherinettes, wear light colours, and dress as a woman however you identify. Make and wear fanciful hats in St Catherine's colours: yellow for faith and green for wisdom.

Eat Cattern cake of cinnamon and caraway seeds, named for Catherine of Aragon, heroine of lace-makers.

Treat yourself to Catherine's taffy or – if you don't mind buttery, sticky fingers – throw a party and pull your own.

28

November

Beginning of the Nativity Fast

(15 November in the Orthodox Julian calendar)

An Orthodox Advent wreath holds seven candles in a ring of evergreen, one for each week leading to the Feast of the Nativity on 7 January.

Each candle is a different colour – or tied with a coloured ribbon – expressing a theme for prayer and meditation

First Sunday ~ Green: faith

Second Sunday ~ Blue: hope

Third Sunday ~ Gold: love

Fourth Sunday ~ White: peace

Fifth Sunday ~ Purple: repentance

Sixth Sunday ~ Red: holy communion

Seventh Sunday ~ White, decorated for baptism

> For unto us a child is born, unto us a son is given: and the government shall be upon his shoulder: and his name shall be called Wonderful.
>
> Isaiah 9:6

30

November

St Andrew's Day

But, far beyond the solar blaze,
  Again I wing my rapid flight;
Again I cleave the liquid maze,
  Exulting in immortal might.
O'er me nor cold, nor heat, prevails,
Nor poison from malignant gales;
I glide along the trackless coast,
That binds the magazines of frost;
Encompass'd by the raging storm,
I smile at Danger's threat'ning form;
I mock Destruction on his tow'ring seat,
And leave the roaring winds, contending at my feet.

Anne Bannerman | *from* 'The Spirit of the Air'

Advent Sunday is the nearest Sunday, either before or after, to the Feast of St Andrew – so it may fall in November.

There will be four Sundays to celebrate before Christmas Day.

Make a simple ring of four candles if you'd like, with a fifth in the centre: one to light each week as they pass.

Weave it with laurel for strength, evergreens for long life, cedar for healing, pine cones for enlightenment.

Hope ~ Faith ~ Joy ~ Peace

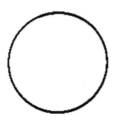

November / December

– Festivals –

that move with the Moon

Here are some of the celebrations that usually occur around mid-November to mid-December – check this year's calendar to find out exactly when . . .

New Moon

Dark, moonless nights are best for star-gazing . . .

Draw on the optimistic, far-seeing energy of **Sagittarius**.
Consider all the possibilities.
Renew your sense of adventure.
Expand your horizons.

Eat simple foods – milk, water, fruit and nuts, soup.

Light a candle at sunset.

Set intentions.
With the new moon: to leave behind the past and
    visualise a hope-filled future.
With the full moon: to focus on long-term goals, higher
    principles and what's to come.

Let go of old and tired things, make space for new and
    exciting beginnings.

In Poland and many Orthodox Christian countries, Advent is a peaceful time of stillness and contemplation, often also of fasting and abstinence. There are moments of prayer each day, and meals are simple.

At this time of year – whether we're heading into the coldest, darkest months or the fiercest, most inhospitable heat – our ancestors would have been quietening down, seeking shelter. It's what the animals do, what the earth does.

How different it might feel, if instead of a rollercoaster ride of social pressures and obligations, we could find a way to have a gentler build-up to the Big Day, with some time for hibernating and restoring as well as bright lights and parties.

Remember, in this season of extremes, to listen to yourself.

Think of your Christmas in layers:
— If you only manage to do one thing, what makes the biggest difference?
— What's the simple plan that everyone can do, even if you're not there to make it all happen like you usually are?
— And if you have a year when you really want to go all out, and have the time and the energy to make all your Christmas dreams come true, what would that look like and what would it take?

~ Chanukah/Hanukkah, meaning 'dedication' ~

An eight-day festival celebrating the eternal power of light over darkness, good over evil.

~

The miracle of the oil – one small jug of pure oil that stayed alight in the Temple menorah for eight days – is celebrated with nightly menorah candle-lighting, special blessings and traditional songs.

The menorah is placed in a doorway or window and holds nine flames: one of which, the *shamash* (attendant) is used to kindle the other eight lights. By the eighth night, all nine candles are lit.

Eat foods cooked in oil: potato *latke* and *sufganya* doughnuts.

Play games with *dreidel* square spinning tops – win matchsticks, pennies, nuts and treats.

Everyone places their bet, then takes it in turn to spin:

Nun/Nit – nothing happens

Gimmel/Gantz – win the whole pot

Heh/Halb – win half the pot

Shin/Shtell – put one in

When the pot is empty, everyone puts one in.

Play until one person has everything – and then redivide the winnings in the giving spirit of the festival!

~

Give *gelt* (gifts of money) to children – or give chocolate coins, to add to the sweetness of the holiday.

Listen . . .
With faint dry sound,
Like steps of passing ghosts,
The leaves, frost-crisp'd, break from the trees
And fall.

Adelaide Crapsey | 'November Night'

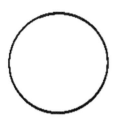

Oak Moon

Woodcock Moon

Mourning Moon

Full Beaver Moon

Deer Rutting Moon

Digging/Scratching Moon

Freezing Moon

Frost Moon

Whitefish Moon

~

Completion ~ Rebirth ~ Reflection ~ Renewal

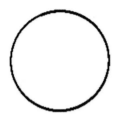

~ Full Moon Festivals ~

~ Xia Yuan Winter Festival ~

Birthday of the God of Water,

who dispels disaster and misfortune

Eat *dousha* buns filled with red bean paste

Give thanks and celebrate the good harvest

~ Loy Krathon ~

Make floating offerings to the goddess of water

An occasion for joy, gratitude and new beginnings

Write your worries on a paper boat and let them drift away

~ Margashirsha Purnima ~

Venerate the moon god

Wear clean white clothes, offer flowers and perfumes

Add basil leaves to your bath water

Find tranquillity

~ Dattatreya Jayanti/Datta Jayanti ~

Celebration of the three gods of Trimurti,
the Hindu male trinity:

Brahma, the creator ~ Vishnu, the nurturer ~
Lord Shiva, the destroyer

Seek purification and enlightenment of the soul and mind, guidance to live a decent life

~ Rainy Seasons ~

As the monsoon season comes to an end in some parts of the world, in others The Wet is just beginning.

The word 'monsoon' is derived from the Arabic *mausam*, meaning 'season'.

> I hear leaves drinking rain;
> I hear rich leaves on top
> Giving the poor beneath
> Drop after drop;
> 'Tis a sweet noise to hear
> These green leaves drinking near.
> And when the Sun comes out,
> After this Rain shall stop,
> A wondrous Light will fill
> Each dark, round drop;
> I hope the Sun shines bright;
> 'Twill be a lovely sight.

W. H. Davies | 'The Rain'

~ Wildfire Time ~

For the Banbai people of the Indigenous Protected Area of Watterlidge in Australia, fire is an important part of the cycle of life.

One Christmas time, when months of drought
Had parched the western creeks,
The bush-fires started in the north
And travelled south for weeks.
At night along the river-side
The scene was grand and strange –
The hill-fires looked like lighted streets
Of cities in the range.

The cattle-tracks between the trees
Were like long dusky aisles,
And on a sudden breeze the fire
Would sweep along for miles;
Like sounds of distant musketry
It crackled through the brakes,
And o'er the flat of silver grass
It hissed like angry snakes.

It leapt across the flowing streams
And raced o'er pastures broad;
It climbed the trees and lit the boughs
And through the scrubs it roared.

Henry Lawson | *from* 'The Fire at Ross's Farm'

Christmas is coming!

Seek bright-red berries
glowing like jewels against stupidly shiny spiked leaves;
gather long twisting tendrils and palm-like
fronds of evergreen
and twine them with twigs of bay;
stud oranges with cloves.

Breathe in the scents of it, fill your eyes with wonders.

Raid your treasure trove of traditions and stock up on memories.

These are the magic days.

But give me holly, bold and jolly,
Honest, prickly, shining holly;
Pluck me holly leaf and berry
For the day when I make merry.

Christina Rossetti | *from* 'Give Me Holly'

*A*LL OF A SUDDEN, it's upon us!

The months of gathering, preparation and anticipation are done, and now it's time to celebrate . . .

Mother Christmas fills Christmas tins with gingerbread, fudge cake, shortbread and flapjacks. Bowls teeter with oranges and apples, kumquats and lychees. Christmas crockery and table linens are washed and piled ready, great armfuls of greenery stay fresh in buckets by the back door. Each morning the post brings a thrill of new cards to be opened.

The Elves are in a race against time with the birds, harvesting boughs laden with berries to be transformed into wreaths and garlands. Menus are planned and food orders are placed. Nothing is left to chance.

It's the time of carol concerts and festive fairs and perhaps you are running yourself ragged trying to fit everything in. Pace yourself, if you can; and make sure you don't miss the magic moments that you're in because you're so busy thinking ahead to what needs to happen next.

Being there is important, being truly present, in that place, in that moment, saving up the memories. So whether you make it in a rush or you get there early enough to see them lighting the candles and hear the whispers and giggles as they wait in the wings, be sure to gather your thoughts into the room with you, and drink it all in.

It can be tempting to try to cram everything in before Christmas. How about buying yourself some time and instead postponing to that strange time when Christmas is over, the parties have stopped and you have peace and space to breathe again. And it might be nice to have something to look forward to . . .

Time of gifts, or gift of time: I hope it's delightful, either way!

~ Decking the Halls... ~

... and tables, windows, front garden, anything you can hang a bauble on.

I have a loft, Mother Christmas had a cellar, and the Elves very likely have a whole dedicated warehouse for storing Christmas decorations.

But the truth is, you don't need boxes of stuff. As with everything, it's about what has meaning for you, what brings you comfort and joy – and what you have the time to do.

Craft if you love to craft; make huge elaborate flower arrangements if you love to flower-arrange; spend an evening with friends weaving a wreath; corral the whole family into Doing the Decorations All Together because that's what you always do; or enjoy the times when they can't make it and you get to hang the tinsel exactly where you want.

While there's something lovely about familiar things you bring out every year, for centuries we were decorating with nothing more than seasonal flowers and greenery before anyone started mass-producing lametta.

Christmas cards

Mother Christmas made the most elegant card-hanging ribbons: perfect bows of forest-green heavy moire silk with one long tail, folded and stitched and pressed to hang almost floor to ceiling from little brass fleur-de-lis hooks that stayed affixed year-round at carefully considered distances around the living room walls, waiting to be adorned come

Christmastime. Cards were attached with golden paper clips at even intervals the length of the silk tail, as carefully selected and curated as though for the walls of the National Gallery.

I tend to just prop mine up wherever I have a clear surface, and then keep propping them back up when they get blown down any time we open the window, or a door . . .

Table decorations

Do you have room in your Christmas stores for special table linens and crockery for just this time of year? Mother Christmas had pieces of Christmas oilcloth for the kitchen table, tablecloths she'd made herself from Christmas fabric bought in the sales, napkins and serving dishes snapped up as seconds or clearance bargains. She loved golden candles and found vintage candle shades. One year as a present I made her some new shades from flame-proof paper, curved into the perfect shape to fit her metal holders and painted with curlicues of ivy.

Nowadays I'm a whole lot more pragmatic about things. But I do have this wonderful piece of fabric – a couple of metres of lush red velvet embroidered with gold and sparkly sequins that I picked up in Deptford Market the first year we hosted Christmas as grown-ups in our own home, and it has filled our hearts with delight ever since. I never did get round to hemming it, and it is the least practical cloth you can imagine for covering a table, but it is The Christmas Tablecloth and once that's unfurled, even if you don't manage to do anything else, the job of table decoration is done.

Laying the table

Things I always forget or don't put out enough of:
Jug of water and water glasses, serving spoons, salt and pepper. That's kind of it. As long as everyone has a knife and

fork, spoon if there's pudding, and the option of a napkin if they want one, the rest of what you do really comes down to whether you like that sort of thing.

For me, it's about what will make things relaxing for us and welcoming for any visitors. Laying things out in advance means you're not flapping about getting things out of cupboards and drawers, but there's no reason you can't just pile it on the side for everyone to help themselves or someone else to arrange into place settings.

A gorgeous spread with candles and glass bowls glinting in soft mood lighting can be breathtaking and add to the magic of a meal, but so can raucous chaos and everyone mucking in together.

Foods that add instant festive feels

Watermelon, pomegranates, persimmons, red-blushed apples, pears, radishes, kiwis, Turkish delight, celery leaves, bay leaves, parsley, citrus fruits, coconut, dusting of icing sugar: choose dishes or add sprinklings of garnish in reds, greens and whites, and your table will feel festive without any fancy decor required.

Finishing touches

Keep floral arrangements and candlesticks low so you can still see over the top of them to have a conversation, and leave plenty of room for the food: that's the most important bit after all.

Over the years, my favourite things have been floating candles or tea lights tucked between long tendrils of ivy that have the double benefit of being both beautiful and slow to catch fire. Choose something that grows abundantly nearby and looks great with minimum primping.

It's kind of lovely to have a signature decoration style – things that are familiar because they come out each year, which your friends and relatives recognise and look forward to seeing and that you don't have to really think about because you know they work.

Have these as your basis, then it won't matter if this isn't the year you feel like spray-painting pine cones and learning modern calligraphy so you can hand write place cards on homemade paper dotted with dried rose petals from your garden . . .

(On the other hand, the years you do have the time and inclination to get crafty, choose to make things that you can use again: those golden pine cones and hand-written place cards could be part of your signature style in years to come . . .)

Seating plan

Mother Christmas always knew exactly where she wanted everyone to sit, and was a genius at pairing up strangers who would discover delightful connections and end the meal as life-long friends. She liked nothing more than to bring together a group of people entirely new to one another and host an evening of discovery for all.

I prefer small groups of familiar faces, quality time with people I know well but don't usually have the luxury of leisurely conversations. I don't think 'boy-girl-boy-girl' seating arrangements feel appropriate these days, and we are all old enough to decide whether we want to sit with our partners or would rather be next to someone we never normally get to see. Formal sit-down dinners aren't really my thing, now I'm of an age when I get to choose.

But it can be daunting and dither-making knowing where to sit. If you're hosting, have an idea in mind of: where you need to be, so you can bob up and down to the kitchen, who's carving and gets to sit at the head of the table as a reward, who needs to be close to the drinks, or get to the loo easily, which relatives want to chat to the young people who will only sit next to them if instructed, that kind of thing . . .

And if you're the guest being told to 'just sit wherever you like', have an idea of where that might be: who would you like to talk to most, do you want to be able to bob up and help clear the plates, or cunningly sit in the seat where you can't get out? Are you up for being the one perched on the stool that's normally in the bathroom, or do you need a proper chair that doesn't hurt your back? Is there a mirror you find disconcerting, or a window you'd like to look out of? And how can you navigate all this gracefully without insulting anyone or coming across as a massive diva?

Crackers

There were a couple of years I remember when Mother Christmas and her friend made their own crackers out of loo rolls carefully covered with crepe paper and bangers bought from craft suppliers. Did they have jokes in? I can't remember. I'm sure there were paper hats, and little gifts. I do remember that they required adult intervention in the pulling: crepe paper is surprisingly hard to tear, it turns out . . .

Crackers each with a little whistle are great, so everyone at the table can play their part in hilariously squawky renditions of carols; or pieces of a game, quiz questions, those impossible puzzles you have to ask Grandpa to solve.

Whoever gets the biggest half wins the prize, and the youngest are sent scrabbling under the table to retrieve those surprises that pinged halfway across the room.

One way or another everyone ends up with a paper crown and a terrible joke.

The tree grew taller every day; and, winter and summer, its dark-green foliage might be seen in the forest, while all who passed would say 'What a beautiful tree!'

A short time before Christmas, the fir-tree was the first to fall. As the axe cut through its trunk, the tree fell with a groan to the earth. It felt pain and faintness, and forgot all its anticipations of happiness in its sorrow at leaving its home in the forest.

. . .

The tree first recovered itself while being unpacked in the courtyard of a house, with several other trees; and it heard a man say, 'We only want one, and this is the prettiest.'

Then came two servants in grand livery, and carried the fir-tree into a large and beautiful apartment . . . What was going to happen to him now? Some young ladies came, and the servants helped them to adorn the tree. On one branch they hung little bags cut out of coloured paper, and each bag was filled with sweetmeats; from other branches hung gilded apples and walnuts, as if they had grown there; and above, and all round, were hundreds of red, blue and white tapers, which were fastened on the branches. Dolls, exactly like real babies, were placed under the green leaves – the tree had never seen such things before, – and at the very top was fastened a glittering star, made of tinsel. Oh, it was very beautiful!

Hans Christian Andersen | *from* 'The Fir Tree'

The word Advent means 'important arrival',
from the Latin *adventus*, 'a coming, an approach'.

How do you like to count down the days?

An Advent candle, marked with twenty-four sections to burn down just a little each night?

An Advent calendar, with the little numbered cardboard doors to find and peel open to reveal what lies behind?

An Advent calendar can be something really thoughtful and special: a little love note for each day, tiny packets to unwrap. We have 'Advent Man'; I found him in a gift shop the summer I was pregnant and I knew he was The One. He is made from soft huggable cotton, is as tall as a toddler and has a long red-and-white striped dress with twenty-four numbered pockets. In each pocket there is a little wooden decoration that is added to the branches of a wooden tree until on the last day a wooden star goes on the top. Recently, chocolate buttons have also appeared in the pockets, as well as novelty Christmas earrings or hair ties depending on how generous or organised the Elves have been.

It's easy to make your own Advent candle too: simply find a pen that writes on wax and mark the sections on yourself. Or fill a jar with twenty-four birthday candles to take out and light each day.

~ Advent Sundays ~

The weekends before Christmas can be days to treasure.

Fill them with treats and lovely things ~ an outing to look at the Christmas lights, or a walk to gather greens for garlands.

Maybe you'll visit Christmas markets and winter wonderlands, catch a panto or join in the chorus at a carol concert.

Take leisurely days to decorate and dress the tree.

Make a ritual of writing and sending cards, choosing and packing up presents.

Fit in visits and parties with the people you won't see at Christmas itself.

Or simply light a candle and have a moment of peace.

December

First Day of Advent

Mark the first day of December by hanging a little something festive on your door. A wreath is traditional, a spiced lavender bag is lovely for indoors, a twist of tinsel adds a simple touch of sparkle. Whatever makes your heart lift when you come home.

Some years you may not have time or access to the right things, or you may just not feel like making your own.

But for those years when you do, making a wreath or garland can be almost meditative – a way of connecting with thousands of years of human instinct to gather and weave and decorate, to collect wild growing things and tame them into an emblem of welcome and delight. And, of course, these days your creativity might stretch beyond evergreens to pom-poms or crochet, tissue paper tassels or origami flowers . . . Craft away to your heart's delight!

Let a morsel of chocolate melt on the roof of your mouth. Choose pure, dark and Fairtrade. Savour it. A little goes a long way, and it has travelled far to reach you.

Feel yourself connecting back through thousands of years to the Maya and Aztec peoples who first discovered this 'food of the gods' and made it a central part of their culture.

Feel yourself connected still to the equatorial families who farm the precious pods which sprout direct from the trunks of Theobroma trees, releasing the cacao beans with a skillful slash of the machete that can only be done by hand.

And you might like to take inspiration from the *chocolatada* parties of Peru: brew up hot chocolate to your own secret recipe with cocoa, cinnamon and orange peel, enjoy with a slice of *paneton* and share with a crowd of happy children.

Unwrap a satsuma.

Plump and golden, satsumas are the easiest to peel of the *citrus reticulata* family – the sweet, small mandarin oranges that grow from blossom shaped like little white stars.

Along with their sisters tangerine and clementine, these little handfuls of sunshine are symbols of good luck and happiness all over the world.

Give tangerines in twos for Lunar New Year – the Cantonese word for tangerine sounds similar to the word for 'luck' and the word for orange is close to 'wealth'; and their bright colour means you're giving gold.

If you have a small star- or heart-shaped cookie cutter, save the peel and cut stars and hearts from it.

Lay your little citrus shapes out on a tray somewhere warm and out of the way and leave them to dry (you can speed up the process by popping them in your oven at a very low temperature for an hour or so).

Add them to potpourri, wire them into decorations, or thread them on strings as gift tags.

She heard the soft rustling flight of wings and knew at once that the robin had come again . . .

She chirped, and talked, and coaxed and he hopped and flirted his tail and twittered. It was as if he were talking. His red waistcoat was like satin, and he puffed his tiny breast out and was so fine and so grand and so pretty that it was really as if he were showing her how important and like a human person a robin could be.

. . .

He opened his beak and sang a loud, lovely trill, merely to show off. Nothing in the world is quite as adorably lovely as a robin when he shows off – and they are nearly always doing it.

Frances Hodgson Burnett | *from* The Secret Garden

3

Victorian posties were nick-named 'robins' for their distinctive red jackets.

Long, long before then, legend has it that the robin earned his red breast as a reflection of his kindly heart.

Come, fill the Cup, and in the Fire of Spring
The Winter Garment of Repentance fling:
The Bird of Time has but a little way
To fly – and Lo! the Bird is on the Wing.

Omar Khayyam | *from* The Rubaiyat of Omar Khayyam

4 December is the feast day of St Barbara, who long ago found consolation in her prison cell by bringing a dried-up cherry tree branch to life, nurturing it each day with drops from her cup of drinking water.

If you take a cutting from a flowering tree today and place it in water in a warm and light-filled spot, by Christmas you will have a 'Barbara branch' of blossoms.

And if it comes into bloom on Christmas Day itself, that's an especially good sign for the times ahead!

It's the Eve of St Nicholas.

Clean your boots and leave them by the door.

Perhaps by morning there'll be a treat inside!

Celebrate Walt Disney's birthday with a movie night!

It is easy to make your own popcorn, so long as you have a saucepan with a snug-fitting lid.

Heat a generous splash of oil.

Scatter in the popping corn, just enough to cover the bottom of the pan. Put on the lid.

Wait . . . Wait.

All of a sudden, you'll hear the corn begin to POP! The lid will judder, shift and shake.

Then all goes quiet. Perhaps there'll be one final burst.

Pop oven mittens on, turn off the heat. Hold the pan and lid and give the pan a little shake.

Tip your fluffy puffs of corn into a bowl and toss with salt, or sugar, or a festive sprinkling of cinnamon.

You could string it into garlands – some folk do – perhaps while you watch your favourite Disney film.

Most likely, though, you'll eat it in big handfuls, spilling some because you always do, still warm from its merry dance inside the pan.

Walt Disney was born on 5 December 1901.

'**I will make** all loving parents my deputies!' cried the jolly old fellow, 'and they shall help me do my work. For in this way I shall save many precious minutes and few children need be neglected for lack of time to visit them.'

. . .

Perhaps you will now understand how, in spite of the bigness of the world, Santa Claus is able to supply all the children with beautiful gifts. To be sure, the old gentleman is rarely seen in these days; but it is not because he tries to keep out of sight, I assure you. Santa Claus is the same loving friend of children that in the old days used to play and romp with them by the hour; and I know he would love to do the same now, if he had the time. But, you see, he is so busy all the year making toys, and so hurried on that one night when he visits our homes with his packs, that he comes and goes among us like a flash; and it is almost impossible to catch a glimpse of him.

And, although there are millions and millions more children in the world than there used to be, Santa Claus has never been known to complain of their increasing numbers.

'The more the merrier!' he cries, with his jolly laugh . . . 'In all this world there is nothing so beautiful as a happy child,' says good old Santa Claus; and if he had his way the children would all be beautiful, for all would be happy.

L. Frank Baum | *from* The Life and Adventures of Santa Claus

St Nicholas Day

Born on this day in the village of Patara in Asia Minor, Nicholas was orphaned young and dedicated the rest of his life – and the whole of his considerable inheritance – to the teaching of Jesus to 'sell what you own and give the money to the poor.'

As Bishop of Myra, he was renowned for his generosity – but apparently liked to give in secret, under cover of night.

His spirit lives on today in the dreams of children that their patron saint will visit with presents.

And – if you live in a part of the world where Santa Claus visits later in the month – today is a good day to get your letter written and sent off to the North Pole!

Noche de las Velitas ~ Night of the Little Candles

Candles dot the windows, balconies, doorways and streets of Colombia, honouring the Virgin Mary on the Eve of the Feast of the Immaculate Conception.

Wear new clothes, if you have them, and make a wish as you light some candles of your own.

Cleanse your home of evil tonight . . .

It is said the devil lurks in dark and dusty corners, under the bed, concealed in piles of rubbish.

Sweep him up and out of your life, build a bonfire and watch it burn.

In Guatemala, the devil is burnt in elaborate *piñata*-effigies, and sent on his way with fireworks, whole neighbourhoods counting down together as the fuse is lit at 6 p.m. precisely.

A more low-key approach might be to bag up all that old clutter and junk you've been meaning to get rid of and take it for recycling, to make room for the Christmas tree.

Write a list of all the things you'd like to let go of, and watch it curl to ash in your candle flame.

The children must have been particularly good this year; for they had never before been given so many wonderful and magnificent presents. The big fir tree in the centre of the room was covered in golden apples, silver apples, buds, and blossoms. Besides that, there were sugared almonds, colourful candies, and many other delicacies. Each and every branch was adorned, and best of all, hundreds of lights sparkled from within its branches like tiny stars. Its warm and inviting glow beckoned the children to pluck its fruits . . .

E. T. A. Hoffmann | *from* The Nutcracker and the Mouse King

~ Feast of the Immaculate Conception ~

Christmas festivities begin for many today:
the tree goes up, a nativity scene is nestled beneath.

If you're lucky, it might even be the day when Tio de Nadal, the Catalonian Christmas log man, arrives.

Feed him sweets and treats, pamper and care for him, tucking him up in a cosy blanket at night, from now until Christmas Eve, when all your hard work will be rewarded with nougat and candies and maybe even a gift or two.

Ring out ye crystal spheres!
Once bless our human ears
  (if ye have power to touch our senses so)
And let your silver chime
Move in melodious time,
  And let the bass of Heav'n's deep organ blow;
And with your ninefold harmony
Make up full consort to th'angelic symphony.

John Milton | *from* 'On the Morning of Christ's Nativity'

Sit still for the length of just one song.

Pause. Close your eyes.

Let the sounds lift you, transport you, remind you that we're all made of stars.

Before the ice is in the pools—
Before the skaters go,
Or any check at nightfall
Is tarnished by the snow—

Before the fields have finished,
Before the Christmas tree,
Wonder upon wonder
Will arrive to me!

10 December is Emily Dickinson's birthday.

Emily Dickinson | 'Before the Ice is in the Pools'

Human Rights Day

Article 1
All human beings are born free and equal in dignity and rights. They are endowed with reason and conscience and should act towards one another in a spirit of brotherhood.

. . .

Article 20
Everyone has the right to freedom of peaceful assembly and association.

. . .

Article 24
Everyone has the right to rest and leisure, including reasonable limitation of working hours and periodic holidays with pay.

. . .

Article 27
Everyone has the right freely to participate in the cultural life of the community, to enjoy the arts and to share in scientific advancement and its benefits.

UN Declaration of Human Rights

Jolly camps and holiday parties all round the beautiful bays of the harbour, and up and down the coast, and all close to home. Camps in the moonlight on sandy beaches under great dark bluffs and headlands, where yellow, shelving, sandstone cliffs run, broken only by sandy-beached bays, and where the silver-white breakers leap and roar.

And Manly Beach on a holiday! Thousands of people in fresh summer dress, hundreds of bare-legged, happy children running where the 'blue sea over the white sand rolls,' racing in and out with the rollers, playing with the glorious Pacific. Manly – 'Our Village' – Manly Beach, where we used to take our girls, with the most beautiful harbour in the world on one side, and the width of the grandest ocean on the other. Ferny gullies and 'fairy dells' to north and south, and every shady nook its merry party or happy couple.

Manly Beach – I remember five years ago (oh, how the time goes by!) – and two names that were written together in the sand when the tide was coming in.

And the boat home in the moonlight, past the Heads, where we felt the roll of the ocean, and the moonlit harbour – and the harbour lights of Sydney – the grandest of them all.

Henry Lawson | *from* The Ghosts of Many Christmases

11

Take a moment to look up at the sky.

The sun, the moon, the stars, guide us even if we don't look to them consciously to show us the way.

Wide open blue or shrouded in clouds, filled to the brim with sunshine or overflowing with rain, it holds us all.

Some leaves of a tree had been found on the nursery floor, which certainly were not there when the children went to bed, and Mrs Darling was puzzling over them when Wendy said with a tolerant smile:

'I do believe it is that Peter again!'

She explained in quite a matter-of-fact way that she thought Peter sometimes came to the nursery in the night and sat on the foot of her bed and played on his pipes to her. Unfortunately she never woke, so she didn't know how she knew, she just knew . . .

'I think he comes in by the window,' she said.

'My love, it is three floors up.'

'Were not the leaves at the foot of the window, mother?'

It was quite true; the leaves had been found very near the window . . . Mrs Darling examined them very carefully; they were skeleton leaves, but she was sure they did not come from any tree that grew in England. She crawled about the floor, peering at it with a candle for marks of a strange foot. She rattled the poker up the chimney and tapped the walls. She let down a tape from the window to the pavement, and it was a sheer drop of thirty feet, without so much as a spout to climb up by.

Certainly Wendy had been dreaming.

But Wendy had not been dreaming, as the very next night showed . . .

J. M. Barrie | *from* Peter Pan

12

Rumours abound, this time of year, about elves and goblins and magical creatures who come in the night and can never be seen; some bent on mischief and some bringing gifts.

Today, it is said, the Jule Lads begin their tumble down from the mountains of Iceland, bringing naughtiness and chaos in their wake. One by one they come each day until Christmas and overstay their welcome until the last one leaves with the Kings at Epiphany.

It seems wise to keep your boots and shoes and stockings neat, lined up beside window, door or fireplace, and to be on your best behaviour, just in case they might pay you a visit and leave you a little sweet treat!

There was an old woman tossed up in a basket,
Seventeen times as high as the moon;
Where she was going I could not but ask it,
For in her hand she carried a broom.
'Old woman, old woman, old woman,' quoth I;
'O whither, O whither, O whither so high?'
'To sweep the cobwebs from the sky,
And I'll be with you by-and-by!'

Anon. | Traditional nursery rhyme

~

Cleaning is a ritual part of any festival, it seems.

13 December – once the last day of the year in Japan – is traditionally the time to begin the *Oosoji* Big Year-End-Cleaning.

Sweep, fold, straighten: prepare your space to be as you would like it to be.

Or settle down with the soot-sprites in *My Neighbour Totoro*!

Santa Lucia, St Lucy's Day

Celebrate light.

A day of thoughtfulness and kindness.

Eat saffron buns – or better still, make them to share.

Wear a garland of candles (or perhaps fairy lights!) in your hair.

~

Sow a saucer of seeds today, tend and water them carefully each day, and your Christmas wheat will sprout in time for Christmas Eve.

Seeds are sprouted for many festivals across the world: Persian Nowrouz and Nepalese Dashain, for example. The custom seems to have originated in Ancient Egypt, where figurines of Osiris, god of the dead, were kneaded from earth, water and barley grains, and placed in tombs to represent resurrection to eternal life.

A symbol of rebirth and the renewal of nature.

14

Pull a cracker, just for the fun of it!

Christmas crackers started life as a sugared almond Bon-Bon nested with a love-note in a twist of bright tissue paper.

Nowadays you can find reusable crackers you can fill yourself, personalised with embroidery for beautiful place holders.

But I can't help feeling it's not a cracker if it doesn't come with a bang and a terrible joke – and the thrill when you're the one left holding the big end, triumphant winner of the rubbishy trinket inside: in that moment, the most precious treasure in all the world . . .

RICE, with proper management in cooking it, forms a very valuable and cheap addition to our farinaceous food, and, in years of scarcity, has been found eminently useful lessening the consumption of flour. When boiled, it should be so managed that the grains, though soft, should be as little broken and as dry as possible. The water in which it is dressed should only simmer, and not boil hard. Very little water should be used, as the grains absorb a great deal, and, consequently, swell much; and if they take up too much at first, it is difficult to get rid of it. Baking it in puddings is the best mode of preparing it.

(Plain and Economical; a nice Pudding for Children.)

INGREDIENTS. – 1 teacupful of rice, 2 tablespoonfuls of moist sugar, 1 quart of milk, ½ oz. of butter or 2 small tablespoonfuls of chopped suet, ½ teaspoonful of grated nutmeg.

Mode. – Wash the rice, put it into a pie-dish with the sugar, pour in the milk, and stir these ingredients well together; then add the butter cut up into very small pieces, or, instead of this, the above proportion of finely-minced suet; grate a little nutmeg over the top, and bake the pudding, in a moderate oven, from 1½ to 2 hours. As the rice is not previously cooked, care must be taken that the pudding be very slowly baked, to give plenty of time for the rice to swell, and for it to be very thoroughly done.

Time. – 1½ to 2 hours. *Average cost,* 7d.

Isabella Beeton |
from Mrs Beeton's Book of Household Management

15

Make yourself a bowl of comfort.

Rice puddings and porridge feature in festive menus across cultures and worlds:

Sweetened with rose water, simmered with spices, dotted with plum jam.

Cooked long and slow and often left overnight to catch the early morning stillness.

Eaten hot or cold, at midnight or sunrise, soothing to children and seasoned with memories at any age.

Or perhaps Angel Delight is more your thing . . .

'Christmas weather,' observed Mr. Elton. 'Quite seasonable; and extremely fortunate we may think ourselves that it did not begin yesterday, and prevent this day's party, which it might very possibly have done, for Mr. Woodhouse would hardly have ventured had there been much snow on the ground; but now it is of no consequence. This is quite the season indeed for friendly meetings. At Christmas every body invites their friends about them, and people think little of even the worst weather. I was snowed up at a friend's house once for a week. Nothing could be pleasanter. I went for only one night, and could not get away till that very day se'nnight.'

. . .

'We are sure of excellent fires,' continued he, 'and every thing in the greatest comfort . . . It will be a small party, but where small parties are select, they are perhaps the most agreeable of any.'

Jane Austen | *from* Emma

Los Posados begins today – a nightly pilgrimage door to door around the neighbourhood between now and Christmas Eve, re-enacting Mary and Joseph's search for somewhere to stay in Bethlehem. There are processions and singing, sweets and *piñatas* – and sometimes even a real donkey.

When fishes flew and forests walked
    And figs grew upon thorn,
Some moment when the moon was blood,
    Then surely I was born;
. . .

The tattered outlaw of the earth,
    Of ancient crooked will;
Starve, scourge, deride me: I am dumb,
    I keep my secret still.

Fools! For I also had my hour;
    One far fierce hour and sweet:
There was a shout about my ears,
    And palms before my feet.

G. K. Chesterton | *from* 'The Donkey'

The first commercial, printed Christmas card was designed on 17 December in 1843, advertised as 'A Christmas Congratulation Card; or picture emblematical of Old English Festivity to Perpetuate kind recollections between Dear Friends.'

On the hither side of the Popham house, and quite obscured by it, stood Letitia Boynton's one-story gray cottage. It had a clump of tall cedar trees for background and the bare branches of the elms in front were hung lightly with snow garlands. As Mrs. Larrabee came closer, she set down her lantern and looked fixedly at the familiar house as if something new arrested her gaze.

'It looks like a little night-light!' she thought. 'And how queer of Letty to be sitting at the open window!'

Nearer still she crept, yet not so near as to startle her friend. A tall brass candlestick, with a lighted tallow candle in it, stood on the table in the parlor window; but the room in which Letty sat was unlighted save by the fire on the hearth . . . Just round the corner of the fireplace was a half-open door leading into a tiny bedroom, and the flickering flame lighted the heads of two sleeping children, arms interlocked, bright tangled curls flowing over one pillow.

Letty herself sat in a low chair by the open window wrapped in an old cape of ruddy brown homespun, from the folds of which her delicate head rose like a flower in a bouquet of autumn leaves. One elbow rested on the table; her chin in the cup of her hand. Her head was turned away a little so that one could see only the knot of bronze hair, the curve of a cheek, and the sweep of an eyelash.

'What a picture!' thought Reba. 'The very thing for my Christmas card!'

. . .

My heart is open wide to-night
For stranger, kith or kin.
I would not bar a single door
Where Love might enter in!

. . .

'Bless the card,' said Dick Larrabee when he went up the narrow parsonage stairs to the room of his boyhood and found everything as it had been years ago. He leaned the little piece of paper magic against the mantel clock, threw it a kiss, and then, opening his pocket-book, he went nearer to the lamp and took out the faded tintype of a brown-haired girl in a brown cape. 'Bless the card!' he said again, with a new note in his voice: 'Bless the girl! And bless to-morrow if it brings me what I want most in all the world!'

Kate Douglas Wiggin | *from* The Romance of a Christmas Card

It was a pretty sight, and a seasonable one, that met their eyes when they flung the door open. In the fore-court, lit by the dim rays of a horn lantern, some eight or ten little field-mice stood in a semicircle, red worsted comforters round their throats, their fore-paws thrust deep into their pockets, their feet jigging for warmth. With bright beady eyes they glanced shyly at each other, sniggering a little, sniffing and applying coat-sleeves a good deal. As the door opened, one of the elder ones that carried the lantern was just saying, 'Now then, one, two, three!' And forthwith their shrill little voices uprose on the air, singing one of the old-time carols that their forefathers composed in fields that were fallow and held by frost, or when snow-bound in chimney corners, and handed down to be sung in the miry street to lamp-lit windows at Yule-time.

Kenneth Grahame | *from* The Wind in the Willows

Sing your favourite carol: belt it out, whistle it, or hum it under your breath.

Find a carol concert happening nearby and carry a handful of small change in your pocket to drop as donations into carol-singers' collection buckets.

Put together a playlist for carol-aoke . . .

19

The poulterers' shops were still half open, and the fruiterers' were radiant in their glory. There were great, round, pot-bellied baskets of chestnuts, shaped like the waistcoats of jolly old gentlemen, lolling at the doors, and tumbling out into the street in their apoplectic opulence. There were ruddy, brown-faced, broad-girthed Spanish Onions, shining in the fatness of their growth like Spanish Friars; and winking from their shelves in wanton slyness at the girls as they went by, and glanced demurely at the hung-up mistletoe. There were pears and apples, clustered high in blooming pyramids; there were bunches of grapes, made, in the shopkeepers' benevolence, to dangle from conspicuous hooks, that people's mouths might water gratis as they passed; there were piles of filberts, mossy and brown, recalling, in their fragrance, ancient walks among the woods, and pleasant shufflings ankle deep through withered leaves; there were Norfolk Biffins, squab and swarthy, setting off the yellow of the oranges and lemons, and, in the great compactness of their juicy persons, urgently entreating and beseeching to be carried home in paper bags and eaten after dinner. The very gold and silver fish, set forth among these choice fruits in a bowl, though members of a dull and stagnant-blooded race, appeared to know that there was something going on; and, to a fish, went gasping round and round their little world in slow and passionless excitement.

The Grocers'! Oh, the Grocers'! Nearly closed, with perhaps two shutters down, or one; but through those gaps such glimpses! It was not alone that the scales descending on the counter made a merry sound, or that the twine and roller parted company so briskly, or that the canisters were rattled up and down like juggling tricks, or even that the blended scents of tea and coffee were so grateful to the nose, or even that the raisins were so plentiful and rare, the almonds so extremely white, the sticks of cinnamon so strong and straight, the other spices so delicious, the candied fruits so caked and spotted with molten sugar as to make the coldest lookers-on feel faint and subsequently bilious. Nor was it that the figs were moist and pulpy, or that the French plums blushed in modest tartness from their highly decorated boxes, or that everything was good to eat and in its Christmas dress: but the customers were all so hurried and so eager in the hopeful promise of the day, that they tumbled up against each other at the door, crashing their wicker baskets wildly, and left their purchases upon the counter, and came running back to fetch them, and committed hundreds of the like mistakes, in the best humour possible; while the Grocer and his people were so frank and fresh that the polished hearts with which they fastened their aprons behind might have been their own, worn outside for general inspection, and for Christmas daws to peck at if they chose.

But soon the steeples called good people all, to church and chapel, and away they came, flocking through the streets in their best clothes, and with their gayest faces.

Charles Dickens | *from* A Christmas Carol

Every time a bell rings, an angel gets his wings.

From It's a Wonderful Life | Directed by Frank Capra
Released 20 December 1946.

Find a bell, and ring it

. . .

Doorbell, sleigh bell, cow bell, hand bell, jingle bells, the little golden bell threaded on red ribbon around the neck of a chocolate bunny, left over from Easter . . .

~ SOLSTICE ~

Nermel Arkhi Khöldönö
~ the time when Mongolian *Shimiin arkhi* vodka freezes ~

With the solstice comes the first of Mongolia's 'Nine nines' – microseasons that measure progress through the phases and intensity of winter cold.

Take a snow day!

Whether it's snowing outside or not, you can make your own white Christmas . . .

Build a mini snowman out of carefully balanced scoops of ice cream, with chocolate buttons for eyes and a scrap of orange peel for a nose. Create a snow scene: melt glacier mints to make sweet little frozen puddles and dust everything with icing sugar.

Stock up the freezer with ice for Christmas drinks: add a sprig of mint or rosemary, if you have some, edible flowers or even a clove or two. Cut up lemons and oranges and freeze the slices.

Listen to your favourite snow-filled songs while you cut paper snowflakes, have a snowball fight with pom-poms or scrunched-up-paper balls. Curl up for a snow-themed movie night: *White Christmas, The Snowman, Frozen* . . .

Make a snowball you can drink.

Fill a glass with crushed ice, add a scoop of melted vanilla ice cream and top up the rest with fizzy lemonade. Mix gently, until the glass feels cold.

Use a cocktail shaker, if you have one, and you could put the glasses in the freezer for an hour or so before serving for the full frosty experience.

If you're feeling fancy, add a dash of fresh lime juice or cordial to your snowball, sprinkle it with ground cinnamon and cocoa powder and garnish it with a shiny red maraschino cherry.

For the boozy cocktail version, swap the ice cream for advocaat or add a measure or two of Mongolian vodka.

And for the full culinary challenge, make your own creamy Dutch custard (with or without brandy) and use homemade lemonade.

Garnish with a slice of watermelon, for immunity against winter's cold and summer's heat, and drink a toast with an old Farsi saying: 'I wish you a long and happy life like Shabe Yalda, sweet as watermelon and fruitful as pomegranates!' – Shabe Yalda is the festival of rebirth held tonight, the longest night of the year in the Northern Hemisphere.

22/23
December

The sun enters tenacious, change-leading
~ CAPRICORN ~
The enduring, irrepressible spirit of nature.

. . .

Month of the
~ OX ~
Loyal, responsible, persistent, sympathetic.

22

Feel yourself grounded to the earth.

Think of the peace of a stable, the scent of the straw, the slow, steady pace of a donkey.

The humble heart.

Clara lay awake some time, for she could not get over the wonder of this new experience of being in bed up here among the stars. She had indeed seldom seen a star, for she never went outside the house at night, and the curtains at home were always drawn before the stars came out. Each time she closed her eyes she felt she must open them again to see if the two very large stars were still looking in, and nodding to her as Heidi said they did. There they were, always in the same place, and Clara felt she could not look long enough into their bright sparkling faces, until at last her eyes closed of their own accord, and it was only in her dreams that she still saw the two large friendly stars shining down upon her.

Johanna Spyri | *from* Heidi

Little Christmas Eve

Look for the brightest star in the sky tonight.

Jolabokaflod

~

The Icelandic tradition
of giving books on Christmas Eve,
then spending the evening reading,
while sipping hot chocolate.

CHRISTMAS EVE

The cottage hearth beams warm and bright,
The candles gaily glow;
The stars emit a kinder light
Above the drifted snow.

Down from the sky a magic steals
To glad the passing year,
And belfries sing with joyous peals,
For Christmastide is here!

H. P. Lovecraft | *from* 'Christmastide'

After supper, Kate started playing the concertina, and the Andersons and Maloneys and several others dropped in. Dad was pleased to see them; he wished them all a merry Christmas, and they wished him the same and many of them. Then the table was put outside, and the room cleared for a dance. The young people took the floor and waltzed, I dare say, for miles – their heads as they whirled around tossing the green bushes that dangled from the rafters; while the old people, with beaming faces, sat admiring them, and swaying their heads about and beating time to the music by patting the floor with their feet. Someone called out 'Faster!' Kate gave it faster. Then to see them and to hear the rattle of the boots upon the floor! You'd think they were being carried away in a whirlwind. All but Sal and Paddy Maloney gave up and leant against the wall, and puffed and mopped their faces and their necks with their pocket-handkerchiefs.

Faster still went the music; faster whirled Sal and Paddy Maloney. And Paddy was on his mettle. He was lifting Sal off her feet. But Kate was showing signs of distress. She leaned forward, jerked her head about, and tugged desperately at the concertina till both handles left it. That ended the tussle; and Paddy spread himself on the floor, his back to the wall, his legs extending to the centre of the room, his chin on his chest, and rested.

Then enjoyment at high tide; another dance proposed; Sal trying hard to persuade Dad to take Mother or Mrs. Maloney up; Dad saying 'Tut, tut, tut!' – when in popped Dave, and stood near the door. He hadn't changed his clothes, and was grease from top to toe. A saddle-strap was in one hand, his Sunday clothes, tied up in a handkerchief, in the other, and his presence made the room smell just like a woolshed.

'Hello, Dave!' shouted everyone. He said 'Well!' and dropped his hat in a corner. No fuss, no kissing, no nothing about Dave. Mother asked if he didn't see Kate and Sandy (both were smiling across the room at him), and he said 'Yairs'; then went out to have a wash.

All night they danced – until the cocks crew – until the darkness gave way to the dawn – until the fowls left the roost and came round the door – until it was Christmas Day!

Steele Rudd | *from* On Our Selection

'Twas the night before Christmas, when all through the house
Not a creature was stirring, not even a mouse;
The stockings were hung by the chimney with care,
In hopes that St. Nicholas soon would be there;

The children were nestled all snug in their beds,
While visions of sugar-plums danced in their heads;
And mamma in her 'kerchief, and I in my cap,
Had just settled down for a long winter's nap,

When out on the lawn there arose such a clatter,
I sprang from the bed to see what was the matter.
Away to the window I flew like a flash,
Tore open the shutters and threw up the sash.

The moon on the breast of the new-fallen snow
Gave the lustre of mid-day to objects below,
When, what to my wondering eyes should appear,
But a miniature sleigh, and eight tiny reindeer,

With a little old driver, so lively and quick,
I knew in a moment it must be St. Nick.
More rapid than eagles his coursers they came,
And he whistled, and shouted, and called them by name;

'Now, DASHER! now, DANCER! now, PRANCER and VIXEN!
On, COMET! on CUPID! on, DONNER and BLITZEN!
To the top of the porch! to the top of the wall!
Now dash away! dash away! dash away all!'

As dry leaves that before the wild hurricane fly,
When they meet with an obstacle, mount to the sky,
So up to the house-top the coursers they flew,
With the sleigh full of toys, and St. Nicholas too.

And then, in a twinkling, I heard on the roof
The prancing and pawing of each little hoof.
As I drew in my hand, and was turning around,
Down the chimney St. Nicholas came with a bound.

He was dressed all in fur, from his head to his foot,
And his clothes were all tarnished with ashes and soot;
A bundle of toys he had flung on his back,
And he looked like a peddler just opening his pack.

His eyes – how they twinkled! his dimples how merry!
His cheeks were like roses, his nose like a cherry!
His droll little mouth was drawn up like a bow,
And the beard of his chin was as white as the snow;

The stump of a pipe he held tight in his teeth,
And the smoke it encircled his head like a wreath;
He had a broad face and a little round belly,
That shook when he laughed, like a bowlful of jelly.

He was chubby and plump, a right jolly old elf,
And I laughed when I saw him, in spite of myself;
A wink of his eye and a twist of his head,
Soon gave me to know I had nothing to dread;

He spoke not a word, but went straight to his work,
And filled all the stockings; then turned with a jerk,
And laying his finger aside of his nose,
And giving a nod, up the chimney he rose;

He sprang to his sleigh, to his team gave a whistle,
And away they all flew like the down of a thistle.
But I heard him exclaim, ere he drove out of sight,
'HAPPY CHRISTMAS TO ALL,
AND TO ALL A GOOD-NIGHT!'

'A Visit from St Nicholas'. Attributed to both
Clement Clarke Moore and Henry Livingston Jr,
first published on 23 December 1823
in the *Troy Sentinel* newspaper.

One more sleep to go!

I had scarcely got into bed when a strain of music seemed to break forth in the air just below the window. I listened, and found it proceeded from a band, which I concluded to be the waits from some neighbouring village. They went round the house, playing under the windows. I drew aside the curtains, to hear them more distinctly. The moonbeams fell through the upper part of the casement, partially lighting up the antiquated apartment. The sounds, as they receded, became more soft and aerial, and seemed to accord with quiet and moonlight. I listened and listened – they became more and more tender and remote, and, as they gradually died away, my head sank upon the pillow and I fell asleep.

Washington Irving | *from* Old Christmas

The wolf also shall dwell with the lamb, and the leopard shall lie down with the kid; and the calf and the young lion and the fatling together; and a little child shall lead them.

Isaiah 11:6

Christmas Day

Whatever happens,
in all the excitement of today,
find a moment of wonder.

There was once a velveteen rabbit, and in the beginning he was really splendid. He was fat and bunchy, as a rabbit should be; his coat was spotted brown and white, he had real thread whiskers, and his ears were lined with pink sateen. On Christmas morning, when he sat wedged in the top of the Boy's stocking, with a sprig of holly between his paws, the effect was charming.

There were other things in the stocking, nuts and oranges and a toy engine, and chocolate almonds and a clockwork mouse, but the Rabbit was quite the best of all. For at least two hours the Boy loved him, and then Aunts and Uncles came to dinner, and there was a great rustling of tissue paper and unwrapping of parcels, and in the excitement of looking at all the new presents the Velveteen Rabbit was forgotten.

For a long time he lived in the toy cupboard or on the nursery floor, and no one thought very much about him. He was naturally shy, and being only made of velveteen, some of the more expensive toys quite snubbed him. The mechanical toys were very superior, and looked down upon every one else; they were full of modern ideas, and pretended they were real. The model boat, who had lived through two seasons and lost most of his paint, caught the tone from them and never missed an opportunity of referring to his rigging in technical terms. The Rabbit could not claim to be a model of anything, for he didn't know that real rabbits existed; he thought they were all stuffed with sawdust like himself, and he understood that sawdust was quite out-of-date and should never be mentioned in modern circles. Even Timothy, the jointed wooden lion, who was made by the disabled soldiers, and should have had broader views, put on airs and pretended he was connected with Government. Between them all the poor little Rabbit was made to feel himself very insignificant and commonplace, and the only person who was kind to him at all was the Skin Horse.

The Skin Horse had lived longer in the nursery than any of the others. He was so old that his brown coat was bald in patches and showed the seams underneath, and most of the hairs in his tail had been pulled out to string bead necklaces. He was wise, for he had seen a long succession of mechanical toys arrive to boast and swagger, and by-and-by break their mainsprings and pass away, and he knew that they were only toys, and would never turn into anything else. For nursery magic is very strange and wonderful, and only those playthings that are old and wise and experienced like the Skin Horse understand all about it.

'What is REAL?' asked the Rabbit one day, when they were lying side by side near the nursery fender, before Nana came to tidy the room. 'Does it mean having things that buzz inside you and a stick-out handle?'

'Real isn't how you are made,' said the Skin Horse. 'It's a thing that happens to you. When a child loves you for a long, long time, not just to play with, but REALLY loves you, then you become Real.'

'Does it hurt?' asked the Rabbit.

'Sometimes,' said the Skin Horse, for he was always truthful. 'When you are Real you don't mind being hurt.'

'Does it happen all at once, like being wound up,' he asked, 'or bit by bit?'

'It doesn't happen all at once,' said the Skin Horse. 'You become. It takes a long time. That's why it doesn't often happen to people who break easily, or have sharp edges, or who have to be carefully kept. Generally, by the time you are Real, most of your hair has been loved off and your eyes drop out and you get loose in the joints and very shabby. But these things don't matter at all, because once you are Real you can't be ugly, except to people who don't understand.'

'I suppose *you* are Real?' said the Rabbit. And then he wished he had not said it, for he thought the Skin Horse might be sensitive. But the Skin Horse only smiled.

'The Boy's Uncle made me Real,' he said. 'That was a great many years ago; but once you are Real you can't become unreal again. It lasts for always.'

The Rabbit sighed. He thought it would be a long time before this magic called Real happened to him. He longed to become Real, to know what it felt like; and yet the idea of growing shabby and losing his eyes and whiskers was rather sad. He wished that he could become it without these uncomfortable things happening to him.

There was a person called Nana who ruled the nursery. Sometimes she took no notice of the playthings lying about, and sometimes, for no reason whatever, she went swooping about like a great wind and hustled them away in cupboards. She called this 'tidying up,' and the playthings all hated it, especially the tin ones. The Rabbit didn't mind it so much, for wherever he was thrown he came down soft.

One evening, when the Boy was going to bed, he couldn't find the china dog that always slept with him. Nana was in a hurry, and it was too much trouble to hunt for china dogs at bedtime, so she simply looked about her, and seeing that the toy cupboard door stood open, she made a swoop.

'Here,' she said, 'take your old Bunny! He'll do to sleep with you!' And she dragged the Rabbit out by one ear, and put him into the Boy's arms.

That night, and for many nights after, the Velveteen Rabbit slept in the Boy's bed. At first he found it rather uncomfortable, for the Boy hugged him very tight, and sometimes he rolled over on him, and sometimes he pushed him so far under the pillow that the Rabbit could scarcely breathe. And he missed, too, those long moonlight hours in the nursery, when all the house was silent, and his talks with the Skin Horse. But very soon he grew to like it, for the Boy used to talk to him, and made nice tunnels for him under the bedclothes that he said were like the burrows the real rabbits lived in. And they had splendid games together, in whispers, when Nana had gone away to her supper and left the nightlight burning on the mantelpiece. And when the Boy dropped off to sleep, the Rabbit would snuggle down close under his little warm chin and dream, with the Boy's hands clasped close round him all night long.

Margery Williams | *from* The Velveteen Rabbit

My true-love gave to me

. . .

A partridge in a pear tree

Two French hens

Three turtle doves

Four calling birds

Five gooooooooooold rings

Six geese a-laying

Seven swans a-swimming

Eight maids a-milking

Nine ladies dancing

Ten lords a-leaping

Eleven pipers piping

Twelve drummers drumming

Traditional | Christmas Carol

The Twelve Days of Christmas

26–31 December

~ Kwanzaa ~

Matunda ya Kwanza ~ First Fruits ~ Harvest Festival

Learning, family, community, culture, celebration.

Remembering ~ Rejoicing

Each day of the African-American festival is dedicated to one of the Ngozu Saba, Seven Principles:

1. *Umoja* ~ Unity
2. *Kujichagulia* ~ Self-Determination
3. *Ujima* ~ Collective Work and Responsibility
4. *Ujamaa* ~ Cooperative Economics
5. *Nia* ~ Purpose
6. *Kuumba* ~ Creativity
7. *Imani* ~ Faith

Scandinavian cultures call these liminal, fallow days Romjul, Juleferie, Mellandagar.

There's a Norwegian tradition of baking and building gingerbread houses, to be smashed and eaten by New Year's Day.

Mother Christmas rolls ribbons, smoothes and folds paper to use again next year.

The Elves shop the sales for next year's presents and decorations.

Get creative with a smörgåsbord of leftovers, eat chocolate and mince pies for breakfast. Pannetone makes delicious bread and butter pudding; fry a jumble of roasties and sprouts in a festive bubble'n'squeak. Dollops of bread sauce, cranberry sauce, brandy butter with everything!

Re-gift, exchange or pass it on: the joy of presents is in the giving and receiving. Be thankful and then let it go.

26 December – 1 January

~ The Octave of Christmas,
the White Octave ~

In the Catholic Church, an eight-day liturgical feast marks the period between the birth and the naming ceremony of the Christ child, with readings, prayers and sacred observations.

26 December – 6 January

Twelvetide ~ The Twelve Holy Nights
~ The Twelve Quiet Days ~

When time stands still between the old year and the new.

Between the moon's year of 354 days, and the solar calendar that gives us 365, there are 12 days which some say lie outside time.

It is a time of peace and silence, of introspection and reflection, looking inward and becoming quiet. Stay home as much as you can, recalling the old year, thinking of resolutions for the coming year, or simply reading, listening, watching and catching up with all the things you rarely have the chance to do.

You might take a moment when you wake up to remember your dreams of the night and what they might mean.

You might take each day as corresponding with a month of the year: to look back on that time in the past, and forward to what you hope it will hold in the future.

26

December

Boxing Day ~ St Stephen's Day

Long before the more modern traditions of rugby matches and hunt meets and First Day of The Sales, Boxing Day was about rewarding those who work hard to help us on every other day of the year.

Known for serving the poor, St Stephen is celebrated on this day, with charity and the distribution of alms. Who would you like to give a bonus to, to reward, thank or support with a Christmas 'box'?

Good King Wenceslas looked out,
on the Feast of Stephen,
When the snow lay round about,
deep and crisp and even;
Brightly shone the moon that night,
tho' the frost was cruel,
When a poor man came in sight,
gath'ring winter fuel.

'Hither, page, and stand by me,
if thou know'st it, telling,
Yonder peasant, who is he?
Where and what his dwelling?'

'Sire, he lives a good league hence,
  underneath the mountain;
Right against the forest fence,
  by Saint Agnes' fountain.'

'Bring me flesh, and bring me wine,
  bring me pine logs hither:
Thou and I will see him dine,
  when we bear them thither.'
Page and monarch, forth they went,
  forth they went together;
Through the rude wind's wild lament
  and the bitter weather.

'Sire, the night is darker now,
  and the wind blows stronger;
Fails my heart, I know not how;
  I can go no longer.'
'Mark my footsteps, good my page.
  Tread thou in them boldly
Thou shalt find the winter's rage
  freeze thy blood less coldly.'

In his master's steps he trod,
  where the snow lay dinted;
Heat was in the very sod
  which the saint had printed.
Therefore, Christian men, be sure,
  wealth or rank possessing,
Ye who now will bless the poor,
  shall yourselves find blessing.

John Mason Neale | 'Good King Wenceslas'

27
December

On 27 December, 1831, 'After having been twice driven back by heavy southwestern gales,' Charles Darwin set sail on the voyage that would revolutionise the way we see the world.

This was the first of many delightful days never to be forgotten . . .

Charles Darwin | *from* The Voyage of the Beagle

28

December

Childermas ~ Innocents' Day

Lullay thou little tiny child,
By, by lully lullay.

O sisters, too how may we do,
For to preserve this day;
This poor youngling for whom we sing,
By by lully lullay.

Herod the king, in his raging
Charged he hath this day;
His men of might in his own sight
All young children to slay.

Then woe is me, poor child for thee
And ever mourn and say;
For thy parting, no say nor sing
By by lully lullay

Traditional | 'Coventry Carol'

29

December

Feast of St Thomas Becket, Thomas of Canterbury

A Knyght ther was, and that a worthy man,
That fro the thyme that he first bigan
To risen out, he loved chivalrie,
Trouthe and honour, fredom and curteisie.
. . .
He was a verray, parfit gentil knyght.

Geoffrey Chaucer | *from* The Canterbury Tales, 'Prologue'

30
December

Any time you spend outside, see what animals you encounter.

Perhaps you can draw on their spirit as inspiration for how you want to be in the year ahead?

31

December

New Year's Eve

Ring out, wild bells, to the wild sky,
    The flying cloud, the frosty light:
    The year is dying in the night;
Ring out, wild bells, and let him die.

Ring out the old, ring in the new,
    Ring, happy bells, across the snow:
    The year is going, let him go;
Ring out the false, ring in the true.

Ring out the grief that saps the mind
    For those that here we see no more;
    Ring out the feud of rich and poor,
Ring in redress to all mankind.

. . .

Ring out false pride in place and blood,
    The civic slander and the spite;
    Ring in the love of truth and right,
Ring in the common love of good.

Alfred, Lord Tennyson | *from* 'In Memoriam A. H. H.'

So may the New Year be a happy one to you, happy to many more whose happiness depends on you! So may each year be happier than the last!

Charles Dickens | *from* The Chimes

Resolu'tion. *n.s.*
[*resolutio*, Lat. *resolution*, Fr.]
1. Act of clearing difficulties.
2. Analysis; act of separating any thing into constituent parts.
3. Dissolution.
4. [From *resolute*.] Fixed determination; settled thought.
5. Constancy; firmness; steadiness in good or bad.
6. Determination of a cause in courts of justice.

Samuel Johnson | *from* A Dictionary of the English Language

New Year's Day

Up in the morning's no for me,
Up in the morning early;
When a' the hills are cover'd wi' snaw,
I'm sure its winter fairly.

Robert Burns | *from* 'Up in the Morning Early'

In the coming year enfolded
   Bright and sad hours lie,
Waiting till you reach and live them
   As the year rolls by.

In the happy hours and radiant
   I would like to be
Somewhere out of sight, forgotten,
   Your delight to see.

But when you are tired and saddened,
   Vexed with life, dismayed,
I would steal your grief, and lay it
   Where my own is laid –

Bleed my heart out in your service
   If, set free from pain,
You, through me, found life worth living,
   Glad and fair again.

E. Nesbit | 'New Year'

1

January

Siku ya Taamuli

Kwanzaa Day of Meditation

Be still.

Be quiet, humble, calm – towards yourself,
and those around you.

Reflect on the three Kawaida questions:

Who am I?

Am I really who I say I am?

And am I all I ought to be?

Every day is a fresh beginning,
Listen my soul to the glad refrain.
And, spite of old sorrows
And older sinning, Troubles forecasted
And possible pain,
Take heart with the day and begin again.

Susan Coolidge | *from* 'New Every Morning'

2

January

It's quite possible that you don't feel ready for the new year, or resolutions, or fresh starts.

In truth, 1 January is only one New Year's Day of many. Judaism alone has four 'New Years' and Sri Lanka's Poya public holidays come every full moon. Lunar New Year celebrated in China, Taiwan, South Korea and Vietnam, is not for a few weeks yet; and many traditions with lunar calendars begin their annual cycle with the March equinox. So there's time if you're not ready yet for the year to begin!

Each new day, week, turn of the moon has its own cycle of renewal, growth and retreat. December's solstice heralds the beginning of earth's harshest seasons: the freezing cold of Northern winter; the scorching heat of Southern summer. It's no wonder if our instinct is to seek the most comfortable place and stay there to wait it out.

Always a night from old to new!
Night and the healing balm of sleep!
Each morn is New Year's morn come true,
Morn of a festival to keep.
All nights are sacred nights to make
Confession and resolve and prayer;
All days are sacred days to wake
New gladness in the sunny air.
Only a night from old to new;
Only a sleep from night to morn.
The new is but the old come true;
Each sunrise sees a new year born.

Helen Hunt Jackson | *from* 'New Year's Morning'

3
January

Perihelion

When the earth is closest to the sun
– falls around 3 January.

    Late lies the wintry sun a-bed
    A frosty, fiery sleepy-head;
    Blinks but an hour or two; and then,
    A blood-red orange, sets again.

Robert Louis Stevenson | *from* 'Winter-time'

I am thankful that in a troubled world no calamity can prevent the return of spring.

Helen Keller | *from* 'Letter to Mrs Felix [Carrie] Fuld'

4

January

World Braille Day

Through the magic of six dots the gates of knowledge have been flung wide, and the blind of each country can enter the world of enchantment beyond the reach of physical sense. Never at any time are we so free as when we hold a beloved book on our knee, and the Braille dots flash into our fingers the greatness, the wonder, the boundlessness of life.

From Helen Keller's draft response to R. S. French containing an address in absentia to read before the Convention for the Blind, 1930

It's time to tuck the Christmas things away.

. . .

Take a moment to think: what was good this year? What would you like to do again? What would you do differently next time?

Think about your future self: what will you be glad that you did today, what will make it easier for you next Christmas?

Write yourself a little note, or card (use the back of one you were sent this year maybe) and put it away with the Christmas things, to find when you get them out again.

5

January

Waes hael – be well! be in good health!

Drink hael – drink well!

Today is twelfth night if you count Christmas as the first night (or you could be truly traditional and celebrate on 'Old Twelvey', 17 January – the date twelfth night would be if calendars hadn't changed from Julian to Gregorian back in 1752).

Drink a wassail to bless the orchards for a good harvest in the year to come – ale, wine or cider mulled with spices and perhaps an egg or two. Share the bowl and raise a toast. Spread fun and good wishes – sing lustily and without a care!

Wassail, wassail, all over the town!
Our toast it is white, and our ale it is brown,
Our bowl it is made of white maple tree;
With the wassailing bowl we'll drink to thee.

Traditional carol | 'Gloucestershire Wassail'

Let today embrace the past with remembrance and the future with longing.

. . .

It was but yesterday we met in a dream.
You have sung to me in my aloneness, and I of your longings have built a tower in the sky.
But now our sleep has fled and our dream is over, and it is no longer dawn.
The noontime is upon us and our half waking has turned to fuller day, and we must part.
If in the twilight of memory we should meet once more, we shall speak again together and you shall sing to me a deeper song.
And if our hands should meet in another dream we shall build another tower in the sky.

Kahlil Gibran | *from* The Prophet

6

January

Twelfth Night

Epiphany

Fiesta de Los Reyes ~ Three Kings Day

Eat King Cake, Galette de Roi – will you be the one to find the prize in your slice, and get to be king for the day?

When you receive this our guests will all be gone or going; and I shall be left to the comfortable disposal of my time, to ease of mind from the torments of rice puddings and apple dumplings, and probably to regret that I did not take more pains to please them all.

Jane Austen | *from* 'Letter to Cassandra'

7

January

Jinjitsu 'Human Day', Feast of Seven Herbs

A holiday of compassion, believed to be the day humans were first created.

According to ancient Chinese tradition, the first seven days of the first lunar month of the year were assigned to a creature:

Chicken | Dog | Boar | Sheep | Cow | Horse | Human

It is said that eating *nanakusa-gayu*, seven herb rice soup, on Human Day will bring health, longevity and good luck. A Chinese custom of eating broth and a Japanese custom of picking green herbs both have the meaning of 'taking the life force of young leaves, which have broken through the snow accumulated during the winter, and putting it into one's body to ward off malicious forces.'

Traditionally the herbs are:

- Japanese parsley (*seri*) dropwort
- Shepherd's purse (*nazuna*)
- Jersey cudweed (*gogyo*)
- Common chickweed (*hakobera*)
- Nipplewort (*hotokenoza*)
- Turnip (*suzuna*)
- Daikon (*suzushiro*) radish

New Moon

Take this month's dark moon as your own private, quiet moment to think about the year ahead.

Eat simple foods.

Light a candle at sunset.

Let go of old and tired things, make space for new and exciting beginnings.

None of us know what the years to come will hold.

Keep looking up at the moon we all share.

Remember, even in the blackest sky, light is only a turn of the earth away.

~ Author's Note ~

The seeds of this book were sown in lockdown, when, like so many of us, I felt adrift, cut off from all those rituals – large and small – that give rhythm and meaning to our lives. As the world seemed to be falling apart, I found myself looking to the constant things: the phases of the moon, the positions of the stars, the sky we all share.

I've always loved an almanac, and now I started to make one of my own. Each month I collected festivals, special dates and wisdom. I put them together in 'moon-cards' that I sent to friends and family, and I began to feel less afraid, less alone.

I found that the World Wide Web was a net I could cast to bring back little treasures of connection. I also realised how biased my algorithms are! Even when travel was impossible, my search engines seemed convinced the only reason I'd be looking was to find my next dream holiday.

What I found instead was an adventure in common humanity.

I'm sure there will be some errors here. I'm not an expert even in the Western Christian tradition I'm so familiar with, and I know I've been biased towards ideas that I'm personally drawn to, regardless of faith or doctrine. I know I'm the product of an education and culture still steeped in colonial attitudes, class structure, patriarchy and consumerism.

I found so many threads that led me to the most surprising connections when I picked them up: stories with beginnings on the other side of the world, shared by cultural traditions that have been and continue to be at war with one another; plants and animals that live, grow and flourish in very different conditions; tiny birds and butterflies that travel unimaginable distances, and have no care for borders or lockdown restrictions or vengeful gods.

So, I confess: my main source of information has been the internet. I take a spark of an idea and seek the answers, which always take me down new and unexpected rabbit holes. I try to find detail that's reliable and comes from someone who likely knows what they are talking about: *The Times of India*, say; or the Australian Government Bureau of Meteorology.

But if the recent past has shown us anything, it's that even the most trusted institutions make mistakes. And what I've learned most of all – because social media, for all its faults, is a miracle of revelation about the real, everyday lives of people – is that we might sing different tunes and make different treats and dance different moves, but all of us express our joy, our hope, our love, through singing, sharing good food and dancing.

~ Community, Generosity, Gratitude & Acts of Kindness ~

A man without charity in his heart – what has he to do with music?
Confucius

Every Sunday in church, my father would tuck his 'tithe' into a special pink envelope and add it to the velvet-lined offertory plate. There are many wonderful teachings and traditions of helping others wherever you look across the world: *Zakat* almsgiving is one of the Five Pillars of Islam; *Danam* charity is considered one of the highest virtues in Hinduism; *Dana* has a preeminent place in the teachings of Buddha; the *Langar* free community kitchen is a hallmark of the Sikh faith; and *Tzedakah* the Hebrew word for charity means 'justice' or 'righteousness' – it is the correct, honest thing to do.

A 'tithe' of 10 per cent of the advance on this book has been shared as donations to the Refugee Women's Association (refugeewomen.org.uk), Action for Refugees in Lewisham (afril.org.uk), Indigenous Literacy Foundation (indigenousliteracyfoundation.org.au), RNIB Talking Books (rnib.org.uk) and Warchild (warchild.org).

~ Acknowledgements ~

My first and biggest thank you has to be to my parents, Malcolm and Polly Bishop, for fifty years of magical Christmases that have set up traditions for many more to come. And to my sister, Olivia, for being my brilliant partner in crime, exceptional cake-icer, genius trifle-maker and creator of the Best Christmas Stockings Ever.

To my husband Simon, and the many hundreds of exquisite mince pies and stollen that he hand-bakes in the Charlton Bakehouse each year.

To my daughter Astrid for giving me the excuse to relive the magic of Christmas through a child's eyes; and encouraging me to actually put my name on the cover of this book!

To Kate (Ma Macer-Wright), Julie-sis, the Macer-Wright clan and Mo-bro. To Jackie, Rosie, Frances, Margaret, Marigold ~ The Mothers of Hertford. To Sophie, Rich and the lovely Pridells. You've all helped Christmases be extra special over the years (not to mention all the other days).

Thank you to my editors Lindsey Evans and Kate Miles, to Caroline Young, Louise Rothwell and all the team at Headline who heard my 'Well, I've always thought it would be nice to do a little Advent-Calendar-in-a-book . . .' idea and have worked so hard to help me turn it into this beautiful creation you're holding now. Special mention to Lucy Rose for the luscious cover illustrations and to Wilf Dickie for infinite patience in translating my jumble of ideas into a visual feast fit for the season.

And thank you to all the friends who sent me such lovely messages in response to my moon-cards; you inspired me to keep on learning about the world. To Marlena Schmool and Ann Eustace, for fascinating correspondence and titbits from your vast stores of wisdom. To Cara Pennock, Emily Luck, Lesley Morgan, Fiona Veacock, Hils Piggot, Ele O'Sullivan, Jo Girdlestone, Lisa Williamson and The Addisons, for all your support and belief in my creativity through these strange times. To Lucy Hale, Louise Stark and Lisa Highton, champions of 'fairy dust'. To Beth Kempton, whose wonderful courses at www.dowhatyouloveforlife.com and personal encouragement inspired me to keep writing. And to The Brum Gang, The Penguin Girls (special mention Maggie Jonessss!), The Hodder Girls and my Charlton Angels: proof that friends are for life, not just for Christmas – even if Christmas is the only time we ever manage to get together these days!

In memory of Tom Luck, Annie Thornley, Matt Richell, Sam Solandt: your creative spirits continue to inspire me.

Most of all, I acknowledge the wisdom and generosity of everyone who shares, champions and advocates for their culture, heritage and traditions, and all who work tirelessly to help bring peace, love and understanding to our world.

~ Bibliography ~

I love the serendipity of research, and for that reason my sources are eclectic and wide-ranging. I might get distracted by an academic paper on how our ancestors measured time and find that in the end it inspires just a word in my own text; or a local blogger will mention a tradition that sends me diving into a whole new strand of rich discovery.

This anthology is compiled from poems and extracts that are in the public domain.

interestingliterature.com and poetryfoundation.org are wonderful sites for exploring poetry, and Project Gutenberg, the British Library's online catalogue (bl.uk) and the Libby library app put classics in your hands at the touch of a button.

I discovered the wonders of BBC Bitesize during lockdown home-schooling and along with the BBC World Service and BBC Sounds I've taken it as a starting point for learning about world religions, culture and history, although always with further layers of research that took me as close to what I could find of the source as I could get, bearing in mind my restrictions of language and UK-centric algorithms.

When I compiled my original lockdown almanac, I worked in shooglebox.com and still use it to collect together all the little gems of inspiration that I find – it's free from ads and distractions and a great way to remember where you first stumbled across something.

And for those who share my love of almanacs, I highly recommend Lia Leendertz's wonderful annual *The Almanac: A Seasonal Guide* and the Royal Observatory's *Night Sky Almanac*.

If you want to follow my trail of discovery about the celebrations and cultural observances that light up our world between September's Equinox and the beginning of the Gregorian New Year, here are some places to start:

Christmas Beliefs and Traditions

Discover a treasure-trove of traditions at whychristmas.com 'Christmas Around the World'
Christkind: German Language Blog 'Forget Santa – meet the Christkind!'
Bethlehem: bethlehem-city.org 'History of Bethlehem'
Christmas Goat: inktank.fi 'How Joulupukki, the Finnish Santa, Went from Naughty to Nice'
El Caganer: shbarcelona.com 'El Caganer: an Unusual Catalan Tradition'
Novena: ewtn.co.uk 'How to Pray the "Christmas Novena" That's Been Said for 300 Years'
Pastorelas: inside-mexico.com 'Las Pastorelas a Centuries Old Christmas Tradition'
Three Wise Men: savellireligious.com 'Tradition and History of the Three Wise Men'
White Christmas: metoffice.gov.uk 'Will It Be a White Christmas?'; Ingalls Weather 'Does Bethlehem ever have a white Christmas?'
Christmas log: barcelonayellow.com 'Tió de Nadal – Caga Tió – Catalan Christmas Log and Song'

Christmas Kit

Dhanteras: pinkvilla.com 'Diwali 2022: 9 auspicious items to buy on Dhanteras to attract good fortune'
Seiso: japanintercultural.com '5S in the Japanese Workplace – seiso: seeing, sweeping and shining'

Christmas music, books and films

My favourite books of carols are:
— *The Easiest Tune Book of Carols*, I & II, compiled and arranged by Eleanor Franklin, Edwin Ashdown Ltd. MCMXLVIII (covered with my childish scribbles . . .)
— *The Golden Book of Carols*, wonderfully illustrated by Treyer Evans, London Blandford Press (inherited from my father who, judging by the hand-written inscription to 'dear little Malcolm, 1948' in the front, was himself gifted it as a child.)
— *Carols for Choirs*, edited and arranged by Reginald Jacks, OUP 1961 (inherited from my mother and steeped in memories of it sitting beneath the hymn book in the hall waiting for Sunday, and her beautiful, distinctive voice singing the harmony beside me in church.)

There are some gorgeous illustrated editions of the classics these days. I particularly love Quentin Blake's illustrations for *A Christmas Carol* (Pavilion Children's Books, 2017), David Roberts' edition of *The Wind in the Willows* (OUP, 2012), Santa Annukka's pocket-sized gift edition of *The Fir Tree* (Hutchinson, 2012), Maurice Sendak's illustrated edition of *The Nutcracker* (Crown Publishing, 1984). My childhood copies of *The Velveteen Rabbit* and *The Happy Prince* are much read, and my battered Puffin paperbacks of *Heidi*, *What Katy Did*, *Little Women* and *The Secret Garden* were essential companions through those strange long weeks of Covid recovery, when comfort reading was an unexpected gift.

And essentials for festive movie nights:
— *The Nightmare Before Christmas* is Tim Burton's stop-frame animation musical masterpiece (and also a great picture book illustrated by Tim Burton, published by Puffin, 1993)
— Also on the Christmas watchlist: *The Muppet Christmas Carol*, *It's a Wonderful Life*, *Let It Snow*, *The Holiday*, *Love Actually*, *Frozen* I & II (preferably watched back to back). *My Neighbour Totoro* is comfort viewing for any time of year.

Festivals and Special Days

Many observances and awareness-raising days have different themes and events each year. Check the organisations' websites for the most up to date information.

A quick internet search will tell you this year's dates for the festivals that move with the moon, and there are many wonderful bloggers and vloggers who will teach you how to celebrate. The Inter-Faith Network of the United Kingdom has a month-by-month calendar of religious festivals at interfaith.org.uk/resources/religious-festivals and see the UN's website for a calendar of Observance Days at un.org/en/observances

Festivals of the Moon

Harvest Moon: jref.com: Tsukimi – the Japan moon viewing festival; CBBC Newsround: 'Harvest Moon: What is it and when will it take place?'; china-highlights.com 'Mid-Autumn Festival (Mooncake Festival)
Full Moon Names: Royal Observatory Greenwich rmg.co.uk: 'Full Moon Calendar'; almanac.com 'Full Moon Names'
Phases of the Moon: tarot.com 'What is the Moonth?'
According to *Esquire Middle East* (William Mullally), Eid al Fitr and Christmas will fall on the same day in 2033.
New Moon: yesspiral.com 'Dark Moon in Libra'; 'Dark Moon in Scorpio'; 'Dark Moon in Sagittarius'; Dark Moon in Capricorn'
— *Mabon House*: 'Moon Lunar Phases for Each Month'

Rainy Seasons

Met Office UK: 'When is Rainy Season?'

Wildfire Time

bom.gov.au 'Indigenous Weather Knowledge: Banbai Calendar'
The author and publishers acknowledge the Traditional Owners

and Custodians of the land. We pay our respects to all First Nations people and acknowledge Elders Past and Present.

Special Plants and Flowers

Diana Wells, *100 Flowers and How They Got Their Names*, Algonquin Books (1997)

Hyacinths: *The RHS* 'Bulbs for Christmas flowering' and *Grows On You* 'Hyacinths for Christmas' reassured me I was remembering my mother's method correctly.

Marigolds: *Times of India* 'Incorporating Marigold into your Diwali decor'

— *The Nue Co*: 'Marigold flowers: from Day of the Dead to Diwali'

Christmas Wheat:

— english.onlinkhabar.com '6 must-know things about Jamar, a key part of Dashain tika'

— en.unesco.org 'Nowruz: The Seeds of a New Day | Silk Roads Programme'

— expatincroatia.com 'How to Grow Bozicna Psenica (Christmas Wheat)'

Christmas Cooking

I owe a huge debt to my mother and sister for the wisdom in these pages. And to help me imagine Christmas feasts on sunny days I turned to

— Donna Hay 'Christmas' on Disney+

— Bill Granger's 'Christmas Day Tips' on YouTube

Presents

Ted-ed: 'What is a Gift Economy? – Alex Gendler' (YouTube)

Otramundialista: 'Mali: Gift Economy' (YouTube)

Wrapping with Furoshiki: *KonMari*: the official website of Marie Kondo has a delightful (of course!) video showing you how to wrap your gifts with beautiful fabric squares. And many happy a moment is to be lost on YouTube marvelling at the artistic talents of dedicated gift wrappers . . .

Advent

Our 'Advent Man' comes from Maileg, Danish makers of irresistible cloth toys. Origins of the wooden tree are lost in the mists of time.
Chocolate:
— Netflix: *The Story of Chocolate*
— pura-aventura.com 'What is La Chocolatada in Peru'
— *Willie's Chocolate Bible: Chocolate Heaven in Recipes and Stories*, Willie Harcourt-Cooze, London, Hodder & Stoughton Ltd (2010)
— *Green & Black's Chocolate Recipes: From the Cacao Pod to Muffins, Mousses and Moles*, Written and Compiled by Caroline Jeremy, London, Kyle Cathie (2006)
Satsumas: Citrus.com, Michelin Guide, Good Fruit Guide, PFAF Plant Database, Science Direct Topics overview of Citrus Reticulata
Robins and Victorian posties:
— British Library: 'The Christmas Robin'
— Blogger M. Morgan Warren at celticanamcara.blogspot.com reminded me of the legend of how the robin came by his red breast.
Jule Lads: icelandmag.is 'Jólasveinarnir'
Oosoji cleaning:
— seattlejapanesegarden.org 'Oosoji Japanese Big Year-End-Cleaning'
— *Tonari No Totoro/My Neighbour Totoro*, written and directed by Hayao Miyazaki (1988)
First Christmas Card:
— postalmuseum.org 'First Christmas Card'
— vam.ac.uk 'The First Christmas Card'
A snowball you can drink: *The Spruce Eats*: 'Traditional Dutch Advocaat – eggnog with a twist'; *BBC Good Food*: 'Snowball cocktail'; *Great British Chefs*: 'Snowball Christmas mocktail recipe'
Jolabokaflod: icelandair.com 'Jolabokaflod: The Christmas Flood of Books'

~ Endnotes ~

All the poems and prose extracts selected for inclusion in the book are out of copyright and in the public domain.

page 1 Anonymous, 'Christmas is Coming', Traditional nursery rhyme.
8 Luke 2:10, *King James Bible* (1611).
20 E. Nesbit (1886–1924), from *The Railway Children* (1906), Chapter XIV.
30 Rabindra Nath Tagore (1861–1941), 'Poems' from 'The Gardener' (1913), *Poetry: A Magazine of Verse*.
34 John Keats (1795–1821), from 'To Autumn' (1819).
39 Su Shi (1037–1101), from 'Water-Accent Song', full poem annotated at LSE.ac.uk.
40 Chiyoji Nakagawa, from 'Proposal on Peace Bell', 1 November 1967 U.N. Ehime Newspaper via peace-bell.com.
43 Sara Teasdale (1884–1933), from 'September Midnight' (1914), *Poetry: A Magazine of Verse*.
46 Lady Mary Wortley Montagu (1689–1762), from 'A Hymn to the Moon (Written in July, in an Arbour)'.
48 Amy Lowell (1874–1925), 'Autumn' (1919), *Poetry: A Magazine of Verse*.
55 Marjorie Pickthall (1883–1922), 'Adam and Eve'.
57 Valmiki (AD 400), *The Ramayana*, Book II, iii. 'The City Decorated'. Condensed into English verse by Romesh C. Dutt (1848–1909).
61 Tao Chien (also known as Tao Yuanming, Tao Qian) (AD 356–427), *from* 'Drinking Wine', full poem annotated at Chinese-poems.com.
66 L. M. Montgomery (1874–1942), from *Anne of Green Gables* (1908), Chapter XVI.
76–7 C. J. Dennis (1876–1938), from 'A Bush Christmas' (1931).
81 George Cooper (1840–1927), from 'October's Party'.
82 Paul Laurence Dunbar (1872–1906), 'Invitation to Love',

The Collected Poetry of Paul Laurence Dunbar (Dodd, Mead and Company, 1913).
- 83 John Clare (1793–1864), 'Pleasant Sounds'.
- 84 M. K. Gandhi (1869–1948), 'Prayer for Peace' (attributed). I have found this in various sources, although none with direct and trustworthy link to Gandhi himself. I hope it is acceptable to include it here, nonetheless.
- 85 St Francis of Assisi (1181–1226), from 'Prayer of St Francis' (anonymous/attributed, earliest known publication 1912).
- 86–7 Susan Coolidge (1835–1905), from *What Katy Did at School* (1873), Chapter XI.
- 88 Helen Hunt Jackson (1830–1885), 'October', *Verses* (1870).
- 90 About World Smile Day, Worldsmile.org/about/about-world-smile-day.
- 91 W. B. Yeats (1865–1939), 'The Balloon of the Mind' (1917).
- 93–5 Oscar Wilde (1854–1900), from 'The Selfish Giant', *The Happy Prince and Other Tales* (1888).
- 96 Qu'ran 'Maryam' 19:22–19:26.
- 99 Quoted (posthumously) in *Time Magazine*, October 1976, no citation given.
- 101 www.glaad.org/spiritday.
- 101–2 Virginia Woolf (1882–1941), from *Orlando: A Biography* (1928), Chapter I.
- 118–9 Genesis 7, 11–8, 22, *King James Bible* (1611).
- 121 Guru Nanak, from 'Asa di Vaar' (Ballad of Hope), Salok Mehlaa 1.
- 126 Edward Thomas (1878–1917), from 'There's Nothing Like the Sun'.
- 142–3 Louisa May Alcott (1832–1888), from *Little Women* (1868), Chapter III.
- 148 L. M. Montgomery (1874–1942), from *Anne of Green Gables* (1908), Chapter XXXVII.
- 149 Laurence Binyon (1869–1943), from 'For the Fallen' (*The Times*, 21 September 1914).
- 150 Robert Louis Stevenson (1850–1894), 'Picture-Books in Winter', *A Child's Garden of Verses* (1885).

152–3 Charles Dickens (1812–1870), from *A Christmas Carol* (1843), Stave Five: The End of It.
157 D. H. Lawrence (1885–1930), from 'Turkey-Cock' (1922), *Poetry: A Magazine of Verse*.
158–9 Mary Seacole (1805–1881), from *The Wonderful Adventures of Mrs Seacole in Many Lands* (1857).
160 The Collect, The Twenty-Fifth Sunday After Trinity, *The Church of England Book of Common Prayer* (1549).
161 Helen Maria Williams (1761–1827), 'To Mrs K, On Her Sending Me an English Christmas Plum-Cake at Paris'.
164 Isaiah 9:6, *King James Bible* (1611).
165 Anne Bannerman (1765–1829), from 'The Spirit of the Air'.
174 Adelaide Crapsey (1878–1914), 'November Night'.
178 W. H. Davies (1871–1940), 'The Rain'.
179 Henry Lawson (1867–1922), from 'The Fire at Ross's Farm' (1894).
184 Christina Rossetti (1830–1894), from 'Give Me Holly'.
191 Hans Christian Andersen (1805–1875), from *The Fir Tree, Hans Andersen Forty-Two Stories* (1930), translated by M. R. James (1862–1936).
200 Frances Hodgson Burnett (1849–1924), from *The Secret Garden* (1911), Chapter VII.
202 Omar Khayyam (1048–1122), from *The Rubaiyat of Omar Khayyam* (1859), VII, translated by Edward FitzGerald (1809–1883).
206 L. Frank Baum (1856–1919), from *The Life and Adventures of Santa Claus* (1902).
210 E. T. A. Hoffmann (1776–1822), from *The Nutcracker and the Mouse King* (1853), translated by Mrs Saint Simon.
212 John Milton (1608–1674), from 'On the Morning of Christ's Nativity' (1645).
214 Emily Dickinson (1830–1886), 'XLV [Before the Ice is in the Pools]', *Poems: Third Series* (1896).
215 From Articles 1, 20, 24, 27 of the UN Declaration of Human Rights, UN General Assembly (1948) Universal declaration of human rights (217 [III] A). Paris.

216 Henry Lawson (1867–1922), from 'The Ghosts of Many Christmases', *The Romance of the Swag* (1907).
218 J. M. Barrie (1860–1937), from *Peter Pan (Peter and Wendy)* (1911), Chapter I.
220 Anonymous, 'There was an old woman tossed up in a basket . . .', traditional nursery rhyme.
224 Isabella Beeton (1836–1865), from *Mrs Beeton's Book of Household Management* (1861), Recipes Chapter XXVII.
226 Jane Austen (1775–1817), from *Emma* (1815), Chapter XIII.
227 G. K. Chesterton (1874–1936), 'The Donkey'.
228–9 Kate Douglas Wiggin (1856–1923), from *The Romance of a Christmas Card* (1915), Chapters I, II, X.
230 Kenneth Grahame (1859–1932), from *The Wind in the Willows* (1908), Chapter V.
232–3 Charles Dickens (1812–1870), from *A Christmas Carol* (1843), Stave Three: The Second of the Three Spirits.
234 From *It's a Wonderful Life* (1946), Directed by Frank Capra [Film]. United States: RKO Radio Pictures. Screenplay by: Frances Goodrich, Albert Hackett, Frank Capra. Based on a short story by: Philip Van Doren Stern.
240 Johanna Spyri (1827–1891), from *Heidi* (1916), translated by Mabel Abbott, Chapter XX.
243 H. P. Lovecraft (1890–1937), 'Christmastide'.
244–5 Steele Rudd (1868–1935), from *On Our Selection* (1899), Chapter XXVI.
246–8 'A Visit From St Nicholas'. Attributed to both Clement Clarke Moore and Henry Livingston Jr., first published on 23 December 1823 in the *Troy Sentinel* newspaper.
249 Washington Irving (1783–1859), from *Old Christmas: From the Sketchbook of Washington Irving* (1886).
250 Isaiah 11:6, *King James Bible* (1611).
252–5 Margery Williams (1881–1944), from *The Velveteen Rabbit* (1922).
256 Traditional Christmas Carol.
262–3 John Mason Neale (1818–1866), 'Good King Wenceslas'.
264 Charles Darwin (1809–1882), *The Voyage of the Beagle* (1839), Chapter I.
265 Coventry Carol, traditional (16th century).

266 Geoffrey Chaucer (c.1340s–1400), from *The Canterbury Tales* (1387–1400), 'Prologue'.
268 Alfred, Lord Tennyson (1809–1892), from 'In Memoriam A.H.H. OBIIT MDCCCXXXIII: 106' (1850).
269 Charles Dickens (1812–1870), *The Chimes* (1844), Chapter IV – Fourth Quarter.
270 Samuel Johnson (1709–1784), from *A Dictionary of the English Language* (1755).
271 Robert Burns (1759–1796), from 'Up in the Morning Early' (1788).
272 E. Nesbit (1886–1924), 'New Year'.
274 Susan Coolidge (1835–1905), from 'New Every Morning'.
276 Helen Hunt Jackson (1830–1885), from 'New Year's Morning'.
277 Robert Louis Stevenson (1850–1894), from 'Winter-time', *A Child's Garden of Verses* (1885).
278–9 Helen Keller, from 'Letter to Mrs Felix [Carrie] Fuld', May 10, 1933, via Helen Keller Quotes on Nature, and from 'Helen Keller's draft response to R. S. French containing an address in absentia to read before the Convention for the Blind', 1930, via Helen Keller Quotes on Reading, American Foundation for the Blind at afb.org.
281 Traditional carol, 'Gloucestershire Wassail'.
282 Kahlil Gibran (1883–1931), from 'The Farewell', *The Prophet* (1923).
284 Jane Austen (1775–1817), from 'Letter to Cassandra', 7 January, 1807.
292 *The Sayings of Confucius: A New Translation of the Greater Part of the Confucian Analects*, Lionel Giles, New York E. P. Dutton and Company (1910), from Individual Virtue.
312 Christina Rossetti (1830–1894), from 'Love Came Down at Christmas' (1885).

~ Index ~

Adam and Eve 54–5
'Adam and Eve' (Pickthall) 55
address books 21
Advent
  Advent kit 23
  Advent Sunday 166, 195
  candles and calendars 194
  daily inspiration 196–9, 204–5, 208–9, 211, 213, 217, 220–2, 231, 235–7, 239, 241–2
  word origin 192
  wreathes 164, 167
Alcott, Louisa May 142–3
All Hallows' Eve 103, 104
All Saints' Day 104, 146
allergies 72
almonds 73
America 104
Andersen, Hans Christian 191
angels 11, 42, 234
animals, inspiration from 267
Anne of Green Gables (Montgomery) 66, 148
Apple Day 97
Aramaic 11
art 99
'Asa di Vaar' (Guru Nanak) 121
astrology 41
Austen, Jane 226, 284
'Autumn' (Lowell) 48

back-to-school 21
'The Balloon of the Mind' (Yeats) 91
Balthazar, King of Tarsus and Egypt 15
Banbai people 179
Bannerman, Anne 165
Barrie, J. M. 218
Baum, L. Frank 206
bay 73
bedding kit 23
Beeton, Isabella 224
'Before the Ice is in the Pools' (Dickinson) 214
bells 11, 40, 234–5, 268
Beltane 106
Bethlehem 11
Bhal Duj 112
The Bible 8, 118–19, 164, 250
Binyon, Laurence 149
birds, migration 80
birthdays
  Dickinson, Emily 214
  Disney, Walt 205
  Gandhi, Mahatma 84
  Picasso, Pablo 99
  Seacole, Mary 159
  Wilde, Oscar 95
Black History Month 82
blossom 203
Bonfire Night 147
Book of Common Prayer 160
books
  Braille 279
  festive list 25
  Jolabokaflod 242
boots 15

Boxing Day 262
Braille 279
brandy 73
brooms 22
Buddha 120
Burns, Robert 271
'A Bush Christmas' (Dennis) 76–7

cakes 159, 160, 163, 283
calendars, Advent 194
camels 11
candles
  Advent candles 194
  Advent wreathes 164, 167
  menorah 172
  moon rituals 50, 107, 170, 286
  Noche de las Velitas 208
  Santa Lucia 221
  scented 75
The Canterbury Tales (Chaucer) 266
Capra, Frank 234
Capricorn 238
carols 12, 230–1, 256, 262–3, 265, 281
Catalonia 104
Catterntide 163
Celtic Tree Calendar 44, 100, 162
Chankillo Solar Observatory, Peru 35
Chanukah 113, 172–3
Chaucer, Geoffrey 266
cheese 73
Chesterton, G. K. 227

chestnuts 104–5
Chesvan 118
Childermas 265
children 151, 206
The Chimes (Dickens) 268
Chinese Zodiac 41, 98, 155, 238, 285
chocolate 73, 197
Choti Diwali 112
Christmas cards
  buying 24
  displaying 186–7
  etiquette 136–7
  first 228
  lists 89
  posting 127, 137
A Christmas Carol (Dickens) 152–3, 232–3
Christmas dinner kit 25
Christmas Eve 97, 243–9
'Christmas is coming, the goose is getting fat' (Trad.) i
Christmas tree 12, 26, 191
'Christmastide' (Lovecraft) 243
Chrysanthemum Day 60–1
cider, mulled 74
citrus fruit 198–9
Clare, John 83
cleaning 22, 23–4, 209, 220
clothes
  Navratri 53
  Noche de las Velitas 208
colours
  Navratri 53
  Orthodox Advent wreath 164
Columbus, Christopher 92

compassion 285
cooking
  cooking kit 24
  preparing and planning 68
  see also food
Coolidge, Susan 86–7, 274
Cooper, George 81
'Coventry Carol' (Trad.) 265
crackers 24, 190, 222–3
crafting 27, 186, 189
cranberries 69, 73–4
Crapsey, Adelaide 174
creativity 99

Darwin, Charles 264
Dashain 221
dates 74, 96
Dattatreya Jayanti/Datta Jayanti 177
Davies, W. H. 178
Day of the Dead 146
decorations 186–9
decorations hanging kit 25
Dennis, C. J. 76–7
Dhanteras 22, 112
Dhia de la Raza 92
Dia de los Muertos 114, 146
Dickens, Charles 152–3, 232–3, 268
Dickinson, Emily 214
A Dictionary of the English Language (Johnson) 270
Disney, Walt 205
Diwali 112, 113, 114
DIY kit 27–8
Dog (Chinese Zodiac) 41
Dominican Republic 129
donations 151, 262

'The Donkey' (Chesterton) 227
donkeys 227, 239
Double Ninth Festival 60–1
driedel spinning tops 173
'Drinking Wine' (Tao Chien) 61
Duchen Festival 120
Dunbar, Paul Laurence 82
Durga 52
Dussehra 52
Dutt, Romesh C. 57

Eid-al Fitr 49
Eightfold Path 120
El Caganer 14
Elder tree 162
electrical essentials 28
elves 13
Emma (Austen) 226
Epiphany 15, 283
equinox 35–8
Erfoud Date Harvest Festival 96
expectations, focus on the important ones 51

'The Farewell' (Gibran) 282
fasting 164, 171
Father Christmas 13
Feast of Seven Herbs 285
Festival of Lights 113
Fiesta de Los Reyes 283
films 25, 205, 236
'The Fir Tree' (Andersen) 191
fire 179

'The Fire at Ross's Farm' (Lawson) 179
fireworks 147, 209
'Fireworks' (a.b.) 147
food
  chestnuts 104–5
  dates 96
  dietary requirements 71–2
  essential ingredients 73–5
  festive colours 188
  gifts 129, 132
  gingerbread houses 259
  herbs 285
  leftovers 259
  rice pudding 224–5
  stocking up 69–71
  tastes 72–3
  traditions and culture 72
'For the Fallen' (Binyon) 149
freezer, stocking up 69–70
fruit 74
furoshiki 133

Gandhi, Mahatma 84
Gaspar, King of Sheba 15
The Ghosts of Many Christmases (Lawson) 216
Gibran, Jahlil 282
gift economy 128
gingerbread 74
gingerbread houses 259
'Give Me Holly' (Rossetti) 184
'Gloucestershire Wassail' (Trad.) 281
glühwein 74

goats 13
'Good King Wenceslas' (Neale) 262–3
Grahame, Kenneth 230
gratitude 10, 176, 292
Guatemala 209
Gurpurab Guru Nanak Jayanti 121

Hallowe'en 103
Hanukkah 113, 172–3
harvest festivals 38, 54, 96, 117, 258
Harvest Moon 38
Heidi (Spyri) 240
help, accepting 139–40
herbs 285
Hodgson Burnett, Frances 200
Hoffman, E. T. A. 210
holly 184
horses 154
horseshoes 103
hosting parties 138–40
housework 22
'Human Day' 285
Human Rights Day 215
Hunt Jackson, Helen 88, 276
hyacinths 45
'A Hymn to the Moon' (Lady Montagu) 46

ice 236
Iceland 219, 242
Immaculate Conception, Feast of the 211
'In Memoriam A. H. H.' (Tennyson) 268
Indigenous Peoples Day 92
Innocents' Day 265

intentions, setting 50, 110, 170
International Day of Non-Violence 84
International Day of Peace 40
'Invitation to Love' (Dunbar) 82
Irving, Washington 249
Italy 104
It's a Wonderful Life (film, Capra) 234
ivy 44

Japan 60, 104, 220, 285
Jesus 11
Jinjitsu 285
Johnson, Samuel 270
Jolabokaflod 242
Joulupukki 13
Jule Lads 219
Juleferie 259

Keats, John 34
Keller, Helen 278–9
Khayyam, Omar 202
King James Bible 8, 119, 164, 250
kitchen appliances/utensils 22
Krampus 13
Kwanzaa 258
Kwanzaa Day of Meditation 273

La Castañyada 104
Lakshmi Puja 112
lamps 112, 113, 117
Las Posadas processions 11
Lawrence, D. H. 157
Lawson, Henry 179, 216
Lhabab Duchen 120

Libra 41, 50
The Life and Adventures of Santa Claus (Baum) 206
light
  festivals of 113
  see also candles
lists
  books 25
  cards and presents 89, 127
  music 25, 231
  things to look forward to 111
Little Women (Alcott) 142–3
Livingston, Henry, Jr. 246–8
Los Posados 227
Lovecraft, H. P. 243
Lowell, Amy 48
Loy Krathon 176
Lunar New Year 198, 275

Mabon 37
Mali 128, 129
Margashirsha Purnima 177
marigolds 114
meditation 273
Melchior, King of Arabia 15
Mellandagar 259
menorah 172
mental health 83, 91
Mental Health Day 91
Michaelmas Day 42
midnight Mass 13
Milton, John 212
mince pies 74
mistletoe 13
Mongolia, 'Nine nines' 236

monsoon 178
Montagu, Mary Wortley 46
Montgomery, L. M. 66
Moon
  festivals that move with 47, 49–54, 57–61, 109, 116–17, 169, 172–3, 176–7
  full moon 57–9, 116–17, 176–7
  Harvest Moon 38
  Lunar New Year 198, 275
  names for November 175
  names for October 115
  names for September 56
  new moon 50–4, 110–12, 170
  phases overview 49
  reflection 286–7
Moore, Clement Clarke 246–8
Morocco 96
Mrs Beeton's Book of Household Management (Beeton) 224
mulled cider/apple juice 74
mulled wine 74
music, festive list 25, 231

Nabanna 117
Nakagawa, Chiyoji 40
Nanak, Guru 121
National Poetry Day 88
nativity 14
Nativity Fast 164
Navratri 52–3
Neale, John Mason 262–3

Nermel Arkhi Khöldönö 236
Nesbit, E. 20, 272
'New Every Morning' (Coolidge) 274
'New Year' (Nesbit) 272
New Year's Day 271–6
'New Year's Morning' (Hunt Jackson) 276
Ngozu Saba 258
Night of the Little Candles 208
The Nightmare Before Christmas (film) 103
Noah and the ark 118–19
Noble Eightfold Path 120
Noche de las Velitas 208–9
'November Night' (Crapsey) 174
Novena 14
Nowrouz 221
nursery rhymes 220
The Nutcracker and the Mouse King (Hoffman) 210

obligations, deciding on priorities 171
Octave of Christmas 260
'October' (Hunt Jackson) 88
'October's Party' (Cooper) 81
office parties 138
oil 172
Old Christmas (Irving) 249
On Our Selection (Rudd) 244–5
'On the Morning of Christ's Nativity' (Milton) 212

Orlando (Woolf) 101–2
Ostara 36
Ox (Chinese Zodiac) 238

Padwa 112
panettone 75
pantomime 14
parties 138–43
'A Partridge in a pear tree' (Trad.) 256
Pavarana 59
pavlova 75
peace 40, 84, 239, 261
peel, candied 73
Perihelion 277
Peter Pan (Barrie) 218
Picasso, Pablo 99
Pickthall, Marjorie 55
'Picture-Books in Winter' (Stevenson) 150
Pig (Chinese Zodiac) 98
Ping'an Ye 97
'Pleasant Sounds' (Clare) 83
'Poems' from 'The Gardener' (Tagore) 30–1
poetry, National Poetry Day 88
popcorn 205
posting dates 127
'Prayer for Peace' (Gandhi, attr.) 84
'Prayer of St Francis' (attr.) 85
presents
  Hanukkah 173
  ideas for 128–32
  lists 127
  shopping for 127, 129, 132, 259

St Nicholas Day 207
  thankfulness 259
  time for giving 132–3
  traditions 128–9
  unwrapping 135
  wrapping 133–4
processions 14
puddings 159

Qu'ran 96

The Railway Children (Nesbit) 20
rain 118
'The Rain' (Davies) 178
Ramadan 49, 96
The Ramayana 57
Rat (Chinese Zodiac) 155
rebirth 221, 237
red cabbage 75
reeds 100
reflection on the past year 261, 280
reindeer 14
Remembrance Day 149
resolutions 261, 270
restoration 171
rice/rice pudding 58, 117, 224–5, 285
robins 200–1
The Romance of a Christmas Card (Wiggin) 228–9
Romjul 259
Rosh Hashanah 54
Rossetti, Christina 184
Rubaiyat of Omar Khayyam 202
Rudd, Steele 244–5

sage 75
Sagittarius 155, 170

St Andrew 165
St Barbara 203
St Catherine of Alexandria 163
St Francis 85
St Lucy 221
St Michael 42
St Nicholas 204, 207
St Stephen 262
St Thomas Becket 266
Samhain 103, 107
Santa Claus 12, 206
Santa Lucia 221
satsumas 198
school term start 21
scissors 28
Scorpio 98, 110
Seacole, Mary 158–9
seating plans 189–90
The Secret Garden (Hodgson Burnett) 200
seeds 221
self-care 111
The Selfish Giant (Wilde) 93–5
'September Midnight' (Teasdale) 43
Shabe Yalda 237
Sharad Purnima 58
shepherds 15
shoes 15, 154, 219
Siku ya Taamuli 273
Sinterklaas 14, 154
sloe harvesting 67
smiles 90
snow 12, 236
Snow Maiden 13
snowball (drink) 237
socialising, party strategies 140–1
solstice 35, 236

Sooty Peter 13
spices 70, 75
Spirit Day 101
'The Spirit of the Air' (Bannerman) 165
spring 278
sprouts 75
Spyri, Johanna 240
stars 15, 240–1
Stevenson, Robert Louis 150, 277
Stir-up Sunday 160
stockings 15, 26, 219
Stonehenge 35
storage boxes 71
storecupboards, stocking up 70–1
sugar 75
Sukkot 54
Sveta Kata 163

table decorations 187–9
Taffy Day 163
Tagore, Rabindra Nath 30–1
tangerines 198
Tao Chien 61
tape 28, 134
teachers 86–7
Teasdale, Sara 43
Tennyson, Lord, Alfred 268
Thadinyut 113
thankfulness 156, 259
Thanksgiving (US) 156
'There's Nothing Like the Sun' (Thomas) 126
Thomas, Edward 126
three wise men 15
Tio de Nadal 15, 211
Tire Sainte Catherine 163

Tishrei 54
'To Autumn' (Keats) 34
'To Mrs K, On Her Sending Me an English Christmas Plum-Cake at Paris' (Williams) 161
trifle 75
true meaning of Christmas 10
'Turkey-Cock' (Lawrence) 157
Twelfth Night 281, 283
Twelvetide 261

UN Declaration of Human Rights 215
UN Peace Bell 40
UNICEF 151
'Up in the Morning Early' (Burns) 271

Valmiki Jayanti 57
Vassa 59
The Velveteen Rabbit (Williams) 252–5
Virgin Mary 208
'A visit from St Nicholas' (Moore & Livingston Jr, attr.) 246–8
The Voyage of the Beagle (Darwin) 264

walnuts 75
washing-up 29
wassail 281
water 176, 178
'Water-Accent Song' (Su Shi) 39
What Katy Did at School (Coolidge) 86–7
White Octave 260

Wiggin, Kate Douglas 228–9
Wilde, Oscar 93–5
Williams, Helen Maria 161
Williams, Margery 252–5
The Wind in the Willows (Grahame) 230
wine, mulled 74
'Winter-time' (Stevenson) 277
witches 103, 124
The Wonderful Adventures of Mrs Seacole in Many Lands (Seacole) 158–9
Woolf, Virginia 101–2
World Braille Day 279
World Children's Day 151
World Mental Health Month 83
World Migratory Bird Day 80
World Post Day 89
World Smile Day 90
World Teachers' Day 86–7
wrapping kit 29, 134–5
wrapping presents 133–5
wreathes 29, 164, 167, 196

Xia Yuan Winter Festival 176

Yeats, W. B. 91
Yom Kippur 54
yule logs 15

Zhon Qui Jie 113
zodiac signs 40, 98, 155, 238

Love came down at Christmas,
Love all lovely, love divine;
Love was born at Christmas,
Star and angels gave the sign.

Christina Rossetti | *from* 'Love Came Down at Christmas'